Transcriptions • Lessons • Bios • Photos

25 GREAT SAX SOLOS

Featuring Pop, Rock, R&B, and Jazz Saxophone Legends, Including King Curtis, Paul Desmond, David Sanborn, Grover Washington, Jr., Kenny G, Sonny Rollins, Chuck Rio, Boots Randolph, Candy Dulfer, and Many More

by Eric J. Morones

ISBN 978-1-4234-1076-8

HAL•LEONARD®
CORPORATION
7777 W. BLUEMOUND RD. P.O. BOX 13819 MILWAUKEE, WI 53213

Visit Hal Leonard Online at
www.halleonard.com

Preface

25 Great Sax Solos is a collection of some of the most renowned and significant saxophone solos ever recorded. The songs themselves are classics: famous, recognizable, and ones you could hear at almost anytime somewhere in the world. These songs will definitely stand the test of time! And fortunately for us, they happen to feature the saxophone (sorry guitarists!).

Of course, when we think of great sax solos, traditional jazz music comes to mind. The collection here, however, presents 25 of the greatest sax solos from the pop music world of the 20th century. Although there are plenty of solos that could have made the list, careful research was done to narrow it down to these, since they are popular, pertinent, memorable, and the ones you hear all the time. And now you finally get to learn them! You'll find solos for both tenor and alto saxophone, though naturally more for the tenor since it's most used in pop music. Also, extensive research was done to provide accurate bios and vital information about the recordings and solos (although in a few instances, this information was simply unavailable).

In order to perform these solos correctly, certain playing techniques are required. They include slight embouchure changes, note embellishments, various articulations, proper air stream, altissimo notes, and an assortment of tone alterations like the flutter tongue and growl. The solos are arranged in chronological order, and each individual playing technique is described in the "How to Play It" section of the first solo in which it is used (you should therefore refer back to these initial discussions when later solos call for the same techniques). Lastly, all of the correct articulations have been notated on the score.

I'd like to personally give thanks to the wonderful musicians who played with me on this project and to all at Hal Leonard Publishing.

Enjoy and good luck!

About the CD

The accompanying CD attempts to replicate the original recordings. Listen, analyze, play along with the solo, and use the tricks and tips described in the text to help you. And of course, please listen to the original recordings for the real deal!

For PC and MAC computer users, the CD is enhanced with Amazing Slow Downer software so you can adjust the recording to any tempo without changing pitch!

The time code shown at the start of each solo transcription indicates the point at which the solo begins in the original recording.

All music on the CD performed by:

Eric J. Morones: Saxophone
Paul McDonald: Piano
Phil Cordaro: Guitar
Matt Spencer: Bass
Bill Wysaske: Drums

Contents

Chuck Rio

From commercials and movies to sporting events and weddings, the song "Tequila" is one of the most inescapable rock 'n' roll instrumentals of all time. Its melody is practically as recognizable as "Happy Birthday." And with that famous melody comes a great solo with a saxophone sound that is unique and razor-sharp.

"Tequila" was written by Daniel Flores (a.k.a. Chuck Rio), who was born in Santa Paula, California in 1929. He first learned to play the guitar, and it wasn't until he was in his mid-teens that he became proficient on the saxophone. In the mid fifties, he made a good living playing in bars and clubs around the Los Angeles area.

In the summer of 1957, Flores teamed up with Dave Burgess, a songwriter and vocalist signed to Challenge Records (a small Hollywood record label founded by Gene Autry). They become good friends and eventually ended up together as members of the Champs. The Champs gave many performances and recorded several songs with Flores, but it wasn't until "Tequila" that they would make music history.

The song "Tequila" was the B-side of the single "Train to Nowhere." Recorded as a last-minute jam, the song became a hit when a DJ in Cleveland decided to play the record.

"Tequila" was based on a Flores-trio stage vamp, and the band basically recorded it as an afterthought. After three takes—with Flores filling the song breaks with his famous "Tequila!" vocal—the song was finished. It was initially just a throwaway B-side for the song "Train to Nowhere," so needless to say the band left the studio having no idea of the enduring classic they had just created!

It wasn't until a DJ in Cleveland accidentally played the wrong side of the record that "Tequila" became a hit. Phone calls quickly flooded the station requesting the song again, and pretty soon it would break nationwide.

The song is credited to the Champs, with Flores listed as "Chuck Rio" in the writer credits. Flores had to assume the pseudonym because he was already under contract as a vocalist with another record label (apparently singing the word "Tequila" three times in the song counted). A legal compromise was later reached in which the other label softened their position in exchange for a half-share of royalties.

By late March 1958, "Tequila" was a nationwide smash. It stayed on the charts for 19 weeks, reaching #1, and later won the GRAMMY® for Best R&B Record in 1959.

After the success of "Tequila," Flores left the band and continued to record through the late 1950s and 1960s. He had a minor hit with the song "El Rancho Rock," but never came close to the success of "Tequila." In 1963, he teamed up with the Persuaders to make the album *Surfer's Nightmare*, which linked his instrumental music with the current surf craze.

After overcoming years of alcohol abuse, Flores continued to play and write music in Southern California. He died on

"I can honestly tell you he never got tired of playing that song."

—Sharee Flores, wife of Danny Flores (a.k.a. "Chuck Rio")

September 19, 2006 at the age of 77 from complications from pneumonia. His greatest hit, "Tequila," has sold more than six million copies worldwide, and is still as popular as ever.

How to Play It

This famous solo is the epitome of raunchy, wailing sax playing! And although it's only 16 bars long, it speaks volumes. To play this solo in the style in which it was intended, one must have a good grasp on some old-school rock 'n' roll sax techniques. The first technique is the growl, which basically involves growling or humming at the same time you play a note. By doing this, you get an aggressive, distorted, and screaming sax sound. Another technique used is the flutter tongue, which is done by rolling your tongue (as if you're rolling your r's) while you play. This is a more aggressive and distorted sound than the growl, and it gives the sax tone a "fluttering" quality.

Note: The growl and flutter tongue techniques are used throughout this book, so please refer back to the explanations above whenever necessary.

The pickup notes and the notes in measure 1 are all played using the flutter tongue, which starts the solo off with a real wail! Rio most likely uses the saxophone alternate "1 and 1" fingering in measure 1 for the A♯ grace notes (to produce the notated A♯ grace notes, hit the F key with your right hand while playing the B). The quarter-note triplet motion over the first three measures gives it a soulful, laid-back feel.

Measures 5–6 feature some quick turns which lay nicely on the horn. Note that beat 3 of measure 5 is a different pattern and rhythm than the pattern played before and after it. Was it intentional, or by accident? In measure 7, Rio quotes the melody of the song. The high F in measures 8–9 are played with the palm keys, and a growl is added to really make it scream! Measure 10 is essentially a trill between palm keys E and F, and ends with an accented glissando on the D in measure 11.

The phrase beginning in measure 12 starts with the flutter tongue again and is carried over into the middle of measure 14. Notice the quarter-note triplet rhythm once again makes the solo feel laid back, and adds a nice rhythmic contrast from the preceding measures. Rio ends the solo with another quote of the melody in measure 15.

This great rock 'n' roll sax solo is usually reproduced note-for-note when cover bands play it, and mastering it is a great way to learn the basic rock saxophone techniques.

Special Tips

Make sure to overblow the horn more than usual to get a harder, more aggressive tone, and experiment with using the growl technique throughout the entire solo. The flutter tongue technique does take awhile to learn and get used to, but with practice becomes much easier.

Photo provided by Frank Driggs Collection

Vital Stats

Saxophonist: Chuck Rio (Danny Flores)

Song: "Tequila"

Album: B-side of the single "Train to Nowhere" – The Champs, 1958; *The Tequila Man* – Chuck Rio, 1998

Age at time of recording: 28/29

Saxophone: King Super 20 Tenor

Mouthpiece: brand unknown (hard rubber)

Track 1

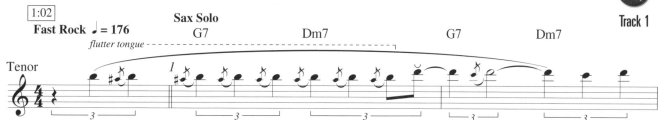

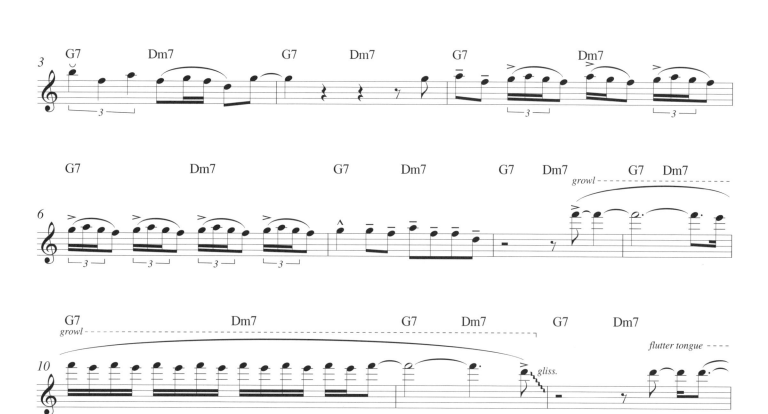

By Chuck Rio

King Curtis

The saxophone sounds of King Curtis can be heard all throughout popular music. His solos and style have been a huge inspiration on how to play R&B, soul, and rock 'n' roll saxophone. King Curtis is so great, we had to cover two of his solos in this book!

King Curtis was born Curtis Ousley on February 7, 1934 in Fort Worth, Texas. He picked up the saxophone at an early age, and started his career playing around Fort Worth. In 1952, he played with Lionel Hampton and soon decided to move to New York. While in New York, he quickly became a busy session player with his trademark honking tenor sound inspired by his main influences Illinois Jacquet, Earl Bostic, Arnett Cobb, and Gene Ammons. He played on many famous recordings like Bobby Darin's "Splish Splash," Ben E. King's "Spanish Harlem," and the hit "Yakety Yak" by the Coasters. "Yakety Yak" went to #1 on both the pop and R&B charts, which led Curtis to later play on another Coaster hit, "Charlie Brown" (#2 in 1959). Curtis would later lead Aretha Franklin's backup band, the Kingpins, when he recorded his famous solo on "Respect" (see page 16).

After recording many brilliant solos for other artists, Curtis was signed as a solo artist for several labels, leading to his own hit R&B singles like "Soul Twist," "Soul Serenade," "Memphis Stew," and "Ode to Billie Joe." Later, in the late sixties and early seventies, he became a successful producer for artists like Roberta Flack and Wilson Pickett.

During his tenure as Aretha Franklin's musical director, and shortly after recording on John Lennon's *Imagine* album, Curtis was tragically stabbed to death outside his New York home on August 13, 1971.

In March 2000, King Curtis was inducted into the Rock and Roll Hall of Fame, and today endures as one of the greatest soul players ever!

How to Play It

King Curtis sets the standard for "saxophone soul" on this solo! In addition, his melodic phrases themselves could make a whole new song! Although the music moves along at a fast tempo, the cut time metric feel makes it seem slower. No matter what tempo, Curtis handles it with ease!

Photo provided by Frank Driggs Collection

"He was a very good jazz player and a very sensitive virtuoso."
—Jerry Wexler, Atlantic Records

The title "Yakety Yak" was used to describe what a teenager would say after being told of their required household chores for the day.

over-accented articulations used throughout the solo. Measures 13–16 contain a great descending line that outlines the chord tones of the A chord, all with legato tonguing.

The second half of the solo, beginning in measure 17, sounds like the first half of the solo, except that it's a little more embellished melodically. Execute the pitch bends on beats 3 and 4 of measure 26 by quickly dropping your jaw downward, like you're saying the word "y'all." Apply these pitch bends on beat 1 of measures 29 and 30 as well.

Special Tips

Notice that all the pitch bends/scoops are done either by bending the jaw down and up quickly, sounding like grace notes, or by both bending the jaw and playing the grace notes at the same time. Make sure to play with a really open sound, over-exaggerate all pitch bends, and use the fast vibrato like Curtis did on the long notes at the ends of phrases. Finally, make sure the time and feel of the solo are on the beat! Practicing with a metronome before you play will help.

Photo © Photofest

Curtis starts the solo with a variation of the opening verse of the song, using a unique way of tonguing known as "staccato tonguing." To do this, you can use a double-tongue articulation such as "ta-ka-ta-ka" on the eighth notes. In the pickup measures before measure 1 of the solo, articulate the two eighth notes and the following quarter note as "ta-ka-toy-ta-ka-toy." When you have a group of eighth notes alone, articulate them as "ta ka ta ka." This way of tonguing produces

a unique sound and articulation, and should be practiced slowly in order to get the hang of it. Also make sure that your intonation is even and consistent while tonguing.

Measure 1 has a long, soulful pitch bend (or "scoop") on the A (beat 2). In measure 2, apply the staccato tonguing on the eighth notes. Notice his fast vibrato that is used on long, sustained notes like in measures 3 and 23, and the

Vital Stats

Saxophonist: King Curtis

Song: "Yakety Yak"

Album: record single – The Coasters, 1958

Age at time of recording: 25

Saxophone: Selmer Tenor

Mouthpiece: Berg Larsen (metal)

Yakety Yak

Track 2

Paul Desmond

Talk about a unique piece! A song written in 5/4 that was popular? Man, try soloing in 5/4… try *dancing* in 5/4! "Take Five" by saxophonist Paul Desmond is a jazz classic!

Born in San Francisco on November 25, 1924, Paul Desmond (Paul Emil Breitenfeld) was the definitive "cool" alto saxophonist. Desmond started on the clarinet at an early age, and eventually went on to study at San Francisco State University. He started playing in various local groups, and soon picked up the saxophone. Desmond was strongly influenced by Lester Young and Charlie Parker (whom he was actually friends with at one time).

Desmond first played with the Dave Brubeck Octet from 1948–1950. After a brief leave of absence, he returned later as a member of Brubeck's new quartet from 1951–1967. This now famous quartet included Brubeck, Desmond, bassist Eugene Wright, and drummer Joe Morello. The Dave Brubeck Quartet traveled the world, won many music

Photo provided by Frank Driggs Collection

The album Time Out, *despite negative reviews, became one of the best-selling jazz albums of all time, reaching #2 on the Pop Albums charts, with the song "Take Five" charting #5 on the Adult Contemporary charts.*

polls, sold hundreds of thousands of records, and was a leading draw on college campuses. In 1959, the quartet recorded the groundbreaking album *Time Out*, which became the first million-selling jazz record (the song "Take Five" was a big reason for this success).

Although the composition of "Take Five" is credited to Desmond, Brubeck explains that the song was a joint effort by everyone in the band. Desmond had written two musical themes, then Brubeck combined the two themes into an A–B–A form. Each member added their own rhythmic ideas and touch, and soon a classic was born! This challenging song, so beautifully crafted, was supposedly recorded in only two takes!

After the huge success of *Time Out*, Desmond quickly gained a reputation for his smooth and melodic musical style. He rarely played solos in double-time, preferring a cool, laid-back style that became known as the "West Coast cool" sound. The quartet later split up in 1967,

"At the time, I thought it was kind of a throwaway."
—Paul Desmond (talking about "Take Five")

and Desmond unofficially retired from music. Supposedly, he didn't play his horn again for three years, and spent most of his time on creative writing (which he studied at one time).

Years later, Brubeck convinced Desmond to play again, and the two recorded an album of duets in 1975. Desmond would also record with Gerry Mulligan, the Modern Jazz Quartet, and guitarists Ed Bickert and Jim Hall (with whom he recorded an album with strings).

Photo provided by Frank Driggs Collection

longer than a quarter note has vibrato applied to it, and also how Desmond keeps coming back to the note F in measures 9–25. Harmonically, it sounds nice since he's hitting the color tones—the 11th and 7th of the Cm7 and Gm7 chords, respectively. Also notice how Desmond uses many variations of articulation; some eighth notes are tongued, some are played with the jazz articulation, and others are tongued tenuto/legato. All the correct articulations are notated in the transcription.

Special Tips

In order to really get the Desmond sound, try to play with less air going into the horn. Make sure your sound and articulations are light, soft and airy, and play with an almost "classical" embouchure. Perhaps a stiffer reed or less edgy mouthpiece will help. A wide, subtle vibrato is also needed, and your technique and embouchure should both be relaxed!

On May 30, 1977, Desmond died of cancer. His legacy surely will be remembered for his unique playing style and the song "Take Five." Today, it remains as popular as ever, and has since become a pop and jazz standard.

How to Play It

Paul Desmond's sound itself is unique in so many ways. His light, airy tone is smooth with a very light, but wide vibrato. His playing is almost like classical "legit" saxophone, and his solos alone could be classical etudes! Desmond's playing technique is incredibly relaxed, making his melodic lines sound that way. Although this may be the first jazz composition and improvisation in 5/4 meter, Paul handles it with such naturalness and ease that you'd almost think it was in good ol' 4/4!

In measures 1–4, Desmond weaves through and around the tones of the chord vamp (Cm7–Gm7) in a way that only he can do! Measures 5–8 feature some nice "call and response" melodic figures that use a light, fast vibrato on all the downbeat Cs. Notice how any note value

Vital Stats

Saxophonist: Paul Desmond

Song: "Take Five"

Album: *Time Out* – The Dave Brubeck Quartet, 1959

Age at time of recording: 35

Saxophone: Selmer Mark VI Alto

Mouthpiece: M.C. Gregory (hard rubber)

Boots Randolph

"Yakety Sax" is that classic song that always seems to bring a smile! Just try to think of something bad while having this tune as the soundtrack—it's impossible! And it's not just because it's the theme song for "The Benny Hill Show"; it's the sax sound and style itself that's so darn happy, thanks to Boots Randolph.

Boots Randolph was born Homer Louis Randolph on June 3, 1927, in Paducah, Kentucky. His father's name was also Homer, so to avoid confusion he was given the name "Boots" from his brother Bob. Boots played a number of instruments when he was young, but finally settled on the saxophone at age 16. He performed in the Army band before embarking on a career as a professional musician. In 1961, he moved to Nashville, where he recorded his multimillion-seller hit "Yakety Sax."

Written by Randolph and James Rich, "Yakety Sax" was inspired by the song "Yakety Yak" (see page 4). After "Yakety Sax" was a hit, Randolph became a star with his combination of Dixieland, jazz, and honky tonk. Along with his unique tone and articulation, Randolph soon achieved what was called the "Nashville sound" with hits like "The Shadow of Your Smile," "Hey, Mr. Sax Man," and "Temptation." He became one of the most sought after studio musicians in Nashville, playing on such diverse recordings as Roy Orbison's "Oh, Pretty Woman," Al Hirt's "Java," and Brenda Lee's "Rockin' Around the Christmas Tree." Boots also made history becoming the first saxophonist to ever play and solo with Elvis.

After years of solo tours and session work, Boots joined the Million Dollar Band—the house band for the TV show *Hee Haw*—and performed on the show for eight years. In the late seventies, Boots opened his own dinner club called "Boots Randolph's," where he performed on a regular basis. He closed shop after 17 years.

In 1996, Boots was back in business, pairing up with brass player Danny Davis. Together, they embarked on a brand new venture in Nashville called "The Stardust Theater," thet featured both artists in concert as well as other major acts.

On July 3, 2007, at the age of 80, Randolph died in Nashville due to complications from a cerebral hemorrhage. The song "Yakety Sax" still remains his signature piece and continues to be popular, appearing in commercials, movies, and scenes that need that funny, happy sax sound.

Photo provided by Frank Driggs Collection

"When I recorded 'Yakety Sax'… that helped me to open a lot of doors to the country music side, you might say."

—Boots Randolph

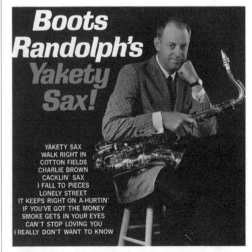

The song "Yakety Sax" has been immortalized thanks to its use on the popular comedy "The Benny Hill Show." Since then, it serves as the perfect soundtrack for any silly or humorous scene.

Photo by Michael Ochs Archives/Getty Images

How to Play It

Boots Randolph is in a category all his own! With the happiest saxophone sound in music, his style and sound are not easy to duplicate. He incorporates a strong mixture of scoops/bends, growls, a hard tone and attack, a shaky vibrato, and an open embouchure. Boots starts his solo with one of his signature licks: a long scoop on the high C♯. Measure 1 of the solo includes staccato tonguing on the eighth notes just like King Curtis did in "Yakety Yak" (see page 4). This type of tonguing is used occasionally in this solo, and is marked "ta-ka-ta-ka" in the transcription; all other eighth notes and quarter notes are played with a long, tenuto tonguing. Be sure to make the staccato notes really short where notated.

In measures 1–4, Boots quotes the famous circus melody "Thunder and Blazes" (adding an extra level of humor), with the melodic lick in measure 7 quoting part of the song's main melody. Measures 9–12 feature a series of fast, scooped glissando runs from middle D up to high D, filling in the octave span with the 2nd, 3rd, and 5th notes of the D major scale. Try to play it cleanly, or else just fly up to the high D notes, making sure to land strongly on beats 2 and 4.

In measures 17–20, we find Boots quoting another famous song, the Irish folk tune "The Girl I Left Behind," which again adds a touch of humor. In measure 23, he repeats the portion of the main melody that he quoted back in measure 7. Be sure to bring out the wide vibrato on the half notes in measures 20 and 24, and really bend those quarter notes in measures 25–28.

The solo ends in measures 31–32 with a fast glissando from middle D to high C♯ (resolving up to D) followed by a leap back down to a short middle D. Don't worry too much about the individual notes of the glissando. Just play the D notes on beats 3 and 1 of the next measure and fill in the space between them with however many notes you want!

Once you learn and master this great solo, you'll be able to put a smile on the face of anyone who needs cheering up!

Special Tips

The Boots Randolph style uses a lot of growling throughout the solo, as well as over-exaggerated articulations that are very precise and short. Keep your jaw and embouchure pretty loose and use that cheery, shaky, "old-style" vibrato a lot.

Vital Stats

Saxophonist: Boots Randolph

Song: "Yakety Sax"

Album: *Yakety Sax!* – Boots Randolph, 1961

Age at time of recording: 35

Saxophone: Selmer Mark VI Tenor

Mouthpiece: Dukoff D9 (metal)

Yakety Sax

Junior Walker

Junior Walker was the one and only Motown instrumentalist to make recordings under his own name. After hearing his solos on "Shot Gun," we can see why! He's another great player who deserved two solos in this book (see page 55).

Junior Walker was born Autry DeWalt Mixon in Blytheville, Arkansas on June 14, 1931. He grew up in South Bend, Indiana, and was so inspired by Louis Jordan that he took up the saxophone in high school. After adopting his childhood nickname "Junior," he formed his first instrumental group, the Jumping Jacks, keeping very busy playing local jazz and R&B clubs. After moving to Battle Creek, Michigan in the late fifties, Junior formed a new band, that became Junior Walker and the All Stars. Together they perfected a mix of raunchy R&B and Detroit soul, with Junior as the front man.

In 1961, the group caught the ear of label owner Harvey Fuqua, who quickly signed the All Stars, allowing them to record a series of raw, saxophone-led instrumentals. In early 1965, Walker and

Photo by William "PoPsie" Randolph
www.PoPsiePhotos.com

the All Stars recorded the song "Shot Gun," which became a big hit reaching #4 on the pop charts and #1 on the R&B charts. The song was also Junior's vocal debut, since the original hired singer never made it to the recording session. It wouldn't be the last time Junior sang lead, nor the last time the band had some hits! Others were "Do the Boomerang," "Shake and Fingerpop," "How Sweet It Is (To Be Loved by You)" (see page 28 for the James Taylor/David Sanborn version), "Pucker Up Buttercup," and "Hip City, Part Two." In 1969, Junior scored another smash hit with "What Does It Take (To Win Your Love)" reaching #4 on the pop charts and #1 on the R&B.

By 1973, the hits dried up, yet Junior continued to record sporadically over the coming years. In 1981, he received an unexpected call and career boost when the rock band Foreigner asked him to play on their song "Urgent" (see page 55). This reminded everyone again that Junior was still a force to be reckoned

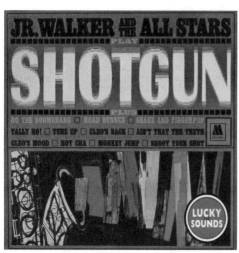

The song "Shot Gun" became Walker's singing debut, since the original hired vocalist never showed up to the session.

> *"I was different, that's all. Instead of singing with my voice, I sang with my horn."*
> —Junior Walker

with! He re-signed with Motown Records in 1983, and continued to play and tour all the way up through the 1990s.

On November 23, 1995, Walker died in Battle Creek, Michigan after a long battle with cancer. Songs like "Shot Gun" and "What Does It Take (To Win Your Love)" have since become R&B standards, with his lyrical style and soulful sounds still continuing to make an impact on saxophonists everywhere!

How to Play It

There are two solos on the song "Shot Gun," and although the first solo could have appeared by itself, the second solo is equally burning!

Solo 1

I can't think of another song in history that starts with a blazing sax solo right off the bat! Talk about setting the tone! The way Walker bends notes and phrases is very similar to how a guitarist would play.

The first solo is very bluesy, with Junior using scoops on all of the palm key notes. He plays with a lot of air and a big sound, punctuated with tight, aggressive articulations. Try to open up your throat and inner mouth more when you play in order to make your tone sound more open and full.

The opening notes and measure 1 should be played very aggressively before leading into a big scoop on the D in measure 2. Junior uses the flutter tongue on the high Eb in measure 3 as well as on the Ab in measure 5. He plays a lot of soulful Bb notes throughout the solo, and although it's usually the tonic of the chord, it's what he does with them that makes them really wail! Make sure to overplay all the written articulations, and make all the scoops wide and big.

Photo provided by Frank Driggs Collection

Solo 2

The second solo has similar melodic lines, but with more note embellishments. As in the first solo, all palm key high notes have scoops on them. Measure 4 sounds almost like a Bb blues scale, where the next measure has a flutter tongue on the high Eb like the first solo. The quarter-note triplets in measure 7 give the solo a laid-back feel, adding a nice bit of rhythmic variety. Measures 8–9 sound bluesy with the lowered 3rd, Db (the "blue" note), emphasized in measures 9–10. Again, Junior plays those tonic Bb notes throughout the solo, also ending the solo on one.

Special Tips

Make sure to play with a wide, open tone that is hard and aggressive, and use the flutter tongue in the places indicated. Also, be sure to over-exaggerate all bends/scoops, and make all the articulations precise and tight!

Vital Stats

Saxophonist: Junior Walker

Song: "Shot Gun"

Album: *Shot Gun* – Junior Walker and the All Stars, 1965

Age at time of recording: 34

Saxophone: Selmer Mark VI Tenor

Mouthpiece: Lawton (metal)

Words and Music by Autry DeWalt

King Curtis

King Curtis strikes again with another classic solo on the song "Respect" (for King Curtis's bio, see page 4). Originally written and performed by Otis Redding in 1965 (#35 on the pop charts), "Respect" was later introduced by producer Jerry Wexler to a young, gospel-rooted Aretha Franklin. In 1967, Franklin's version of the song went to #1, and quickly became one of her signature songs. More recently, it was listed #5 on *Rolling Stone* magazine's 500 Greatest Songs. Due to Franklin's huge success with "Respect," Redding always referred to it as "the song Aretha took away from me!"

Aretha Louise Franklin was born March 25, 1942 in Memphis, Tennessee. Her father was a popular preacher, and she credits his sermons for her strong sense of timing. She taught herself how to play the piano at age eight, and cut her first records when she was 14. In 1960, Franklin moved to New York where she took dance and singing lessons. Soon after, she signed with Columbia Records. But it was with Atlantic Records that she would leave her mark on music forever. Her first album for Atlantic, *I Never Loved a Man the Way I Love You*, became an instant classic (especially because it had "Respect" on it). On her version of the song, a bridge was added, said to be based on the chord changes of "When Something Is Wrong with My Baby" by the soul duo Sam and Dave. (It has also been said that King Curtis's solo may have been lifted from this song, too.) Besides "Respect," Aretha would have many more hits, such as "Think," "(You Make Me Feel Like) A Natural Woman," "Chain of Fools," "Call Me," and the 1985 success "Freeway of Love."

As of 2006, the legendary "Queen of Soul" has received 17 GRAMMY® Awards, has been inducted into the Rock and Roll Hall of Fame, and continues to perform and inspire many vocalists today as one of the greatest voices in music history!

Photo provided by Frank Driggs Collection

After recording with Columbia Records for five years, Aretha's masterpiece I Never Loved a Man the Way I Love You *was her debut album for Atlantic Records. It has since become a soul landmark!*

"If a song's about something I've experienced, or that could've happened to me, it's good. But if it's alien to me, I couldn't lend anything to it because that's what soul is all about."
—Aretha Franklin

Photo provided by Frank Driggs Collection

In measures 3–4, the harmony changes to a C# chord, so Curtis naturally shifts to the C# major pentatonic scale starting on the 3rd. Notice how the grace notes in these measures add a nice rhythmic texture to the solo. Measures 5–6 recap the first two measures of the solo with some slight melodic variations. In measure 7, Curtis comes in with the most interesting line of the solo, featuring an A blues scale–like pattern (with grace notes) that starts on an altissimo G (see fingering below the transcription). The grace notes thrown in make it especially challenging to play the rhythms correctly. Finally, the solo ends with one soulful line as Curtis plays an aggressive ascending phrase with a big growl, and a large scoop on the C#.

Special Tips

Play the solo with aggression using tight, strong articulations, and make all the bends wide and deep. Also, try growling through the whole solo to really make it mean and dirty!

How to Play It

Once again, King Curtis uses his unique sound and style to grace this classic song! Melodically and rhythmically, his solos look and sound like no other. In particular, his use of grace notes and syncopated rhythms enlivened with scattered flurries of notes make this solo a King Curtis original! Also, the song's jazzy chord changes suit Curtis's playing perfectly.

Curtis begins his solo with a nice ascending line (almost a minor pentatonic scale) which features a flawlessly executed leap up to the altissimo G# (the fingering is given below the transcription). Curtis ends the lick by highlighting the final G# in measure 2 with a wide vibrato.

Vital Stats

Saxophonist: King Curtis

Song: "Respect"

Album: *I Never Loved a Man the Way I Love You –* Aretha Franklin, 1967

Age at time of recording: 33

Saxophone: Selmer Tenor

Mouthpiece: Berg Larsen (metal)

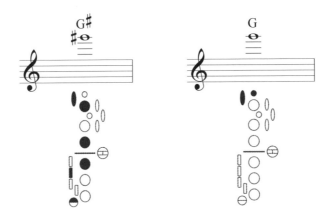

Words and Music by Otis Redding
Copyright © 1965 IRVING MUSIC, INC.
Copyright Renewed
All Rights Reserved   Used by Permission

Mike Shapiro

The solo on "Spooky," recorded by the Classics IV, is perhaps the most controversial of the bunch due to the mystery surrounding the identity of the soloist who played it. Several musicians over the years claimed to have played the solo, but I believe we can now put it to rest that it was indeed Mike Shapiro who played this great solo. Joe Glickman, biographer and archivist for the Classics IV, has graciously provided photos, history, and insight into this music mystery, and has also written and produced a documentary about the band called "The Fifth Classic," in which the elusive Mike Shapiro himself is interviewed.

Michael P. Shapiro was born January 3rd, 1940 in Atlanta, Georgia. Mike took up the saxophone and went on to become an in-demand session player in the 1960s Atlanta recording scene. His sax playing has graced the recordings of the Classics IV, Stevie Wonder, and Dionne Warwick (to name but a few), and his music has since been recorded by artists such as Boots Randolph (see "Yakety Sax"), Dusty Springfield, Lawrence Welk, and

The original album Spooky *features 11 songs, but all together they total less than 26 minutes in length.*

David Sanborn (see "How Sweet It Is (To Be Loved by You)").

Mike Shapiro and Harry Middlebrooks originally penned an instrumental version of "Spooky." As Mike recalls, "Harry M. and I wrote it at a club called 'The Houndstooth' in Atlanta. There was this girl that was singing with us and she was doing 'Summertime.' I played this lick at the end of the song and I turned to Harry and said, 'We'll write a song out of that.' I just happened to feel that first chord, a sharp 9. It was really doubling the minor 3rd. So, I went over to the piano and played it. Harry put the other chord to the song, which could be construed as a 13 or a 6th chord. It's a simple song; a minor key blues is all it is." The duo recorded the song with Mike on tenor sax and Harry on organ. "I heard the demo we did and thought the alto wasn't quite full enough... so I played the tenor sax, which wasn't really my instrument, but I was trying to play for the best sound we could get," recalls Shapiro.

"I had originally thought of calling the song 'Boss,'" Shapiro remarks, "But Mr. Lowery [the publisher] said that didn't necessarily do it for him, so after asking my wife what she thought about the tape we recorded, she said, 'Well, I think it was spooky.' Then I go to work that night and the drummer said the same thing, so I said, 'I believe that's what the name of the song should be called.'" "Spooky" was released as a single in 1966, then later released on an LP titled *The Spooky Sound of Mike Sharpe*. Mike went by

Photo courtesy of Joe Glickman/The Classics IV

"I can say with one-hundred percent certainty that Mike Shapiro is the sax player on 'Spooky.'"

—Joe Glickman, biographer and archivist for the Classics IV

the last name "Sharpe" to appease the management's desire for a more commercial-sounding moniker. When asked about the name change, producer Buddy Buie chuckled, "It wasn't 'gentile' enough." The "Spooky" instrumental went on to some success as a regional hit, but a few years later, fate intervened as the Classics IV entered the picture.

Photo courtesy of Joe Glickman/The Classics IV

The Classics IV created a unique sound of rock in the late 1960s and early 1970s. Drummer and singer Dennis Yost was in a band called Leroy and the Moments in Jacksonville, Florida. When the group wanted to make personnel and musical changes, they decided on the name the Classics (coming from Yost's Classic-model drum kit). After being threatened legally by a band already going by the Classics name, the group became the Four Classics, and later the Classics IV. The band eventually signed with the Lowery Music Group—the same publishing company that launched Shapiro's "Spooky"—who helped them land a recording contract with Capitol Records. Guitarist J.R. Cobb heard "Spooky" and decided to add lyrics and re-record it with Shapiro playing the saxophone solo. The new version received frequent airplay by a radio station in Louisville, Kentucky, and soon it spread across the nation, reaching #3 on the charts in early 1968 (#46 in the

U.K.). The Classics IV had hit it big and continued to score hits with songs like "Traces" and "Stormy."

Shapiro never toured or performed live with the Classics IV. "They were gonna try to promote me as a recording artist, but the problem was I was in love with my wife at the time and I knew how difficult, to a certain degree, it is to make it in music and I wasn't really interested in fame," says Shapiro. "People love the song and I'm glad they do. That song has fed me and quite a few different folk for four decades. It's a phenomenon to me."

Mike Shapiro is also responsible for the sax solos on other Classics IV records including *Soul Train*, *Where Did All the Good Times Go*, and *Time for Love*. In addition, Shapiro (as Mike Sharpe) recorded albums for Liberty Records such as *Sharpest Sax* and *Mystic Light*. He currently resides in Atlanta, Georgia, while lead singer Dennis Yost continues to perform and tour under the Classics IV name.

How to Play It

The sax solo on this rock classic is perfect! It's not flashy, but simple, soulful, groovy, and it fits the song perfectly! Shapiro plays the sax very aggressively, with a big, gruff, bright tone that's certainly unique sounding. The beginning of the solo features a nice

G blues lick in measures 1–3. Make sure to play the wide vibrato on the G in the first measure, and notice that a wide and rapid vibrato occurs on all the notes that are a quarter note value or longer. Heavy accents should be played throughout measures 4–8, particularly in measures 5–6 where there is a nice syncopated pattern that arpeggiates the 3rd, 5th, and 7th of the Gm7 chord. Bring out the accents on beats 1 and 2 of measure 12 before playing the glissando from the B♭ up to the altissimo G (see the fingering below the transcription). You'll find that most of the solo is very diatonic and hovers around the notes G and B♭, however, in the bluesy ending, Shapiro incorporates C♯ and D♭ in measures 13–14, which is very tasteful.

Special Tips

This solo really needs that big, open sound! Overblow the horn more than usual to get a harder, more open sound, and relax your embouchure as well. Also don't forget to use a rapid vibrato on the notes indicated, and articulate all accents strongly.

Vital Stats

Saxophonist: Mike Shapiro

Song: "Spooky"

Album: *Spooky –* The Classics IV, 1968

Age at time of recording: 28

Saxophone: unknown

Mouthpiece: unknown

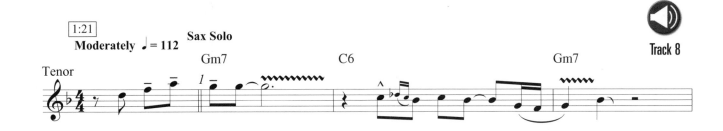

Tenor

Wild Bill Moore

Photo provided by Frank Driggs Collection

"Music is one of the closest link-ups with God that we can probably experience. I think it's a common vibrating tone of the musical notes that holds all life together."

—Marvin Gaye

"Mercy Mercy Me (The Ecology)" is one of music's greatest songs! The second single off Marvin Gaye's legendary 1971 album *What's Going On*, it features a wailing sax solo by Wild Bill Moore.

Marvin Gaye (Marvin Pentz Gay, Jr.) was born on April 2, 1939 in Washington, D.C. This soul/R&B singer, songwriter, and producer, had numerous hits like "Stubborn Kind of Fellow," "How Sweet It Is (To Be Loved by You)," "I Heard It Through the Grapevine," "Let's Get It On," and "Sexual Healing." In 1971, Gaye composed "What's Going On" for his album of the same name. Motown's Barry Gordy initially didn't want to release the single, believing it had no hit potential. Eventually it was released and became a surprise hit. The heavily political album is now considered to be one of the greatest records of all time. The second single, "Mercy Mercy Me (The Ecology)," became a famous and poignant anthem of sorrow on the world dealing with the environment. The song rose to #4 on the pop charts and hit #1 on the R&B singles charts in August of 1971, quickly becoming the second million-copy seller from the album.

After several ups and downs from drug addiction over the years, Gaye was on the comeback trail with his 1982 hit "Sexual Healing," and his amazing performance of "The Star Spangled Banner" at the 1983 NBA All-Star Game. Tragically, on April 1, 1984, Gaye was shot and killed by his father during an argument.

In 2002, "Mercy Mercy Me (The Ecology)" became Gaye's third single to win a GRAMMY® Hall of Fame Award. The song's political stance remains valid today, and it has become a timeless classic!

Saxophonist Wild Bill Moore (William M. Moore) was born in Houston, Texas on June 13, 1918. He took up the sax early in life, and was highly influenced by Chu Berry. He was at one time even a boxer, becoming Michigan's amateur Golden Gloves Light-Heavyweight Champ in 1937. He later turned pro, but ended up returning back to music.

Moore musically made his mark in Chicago in 1944 while playing on recordings with vocalist Christine Chatman. He later played with the Slim Gaillard Orchestra and Red Allan, and finally recorded on his own for the Apollo label in 1945. In 1948, Moore cracked the charts with the song "We're Gonna Rock, We're Gonna Roll," which lasted one week at #14 (he was credited with lead vocals as well as tenor sax).

Moore became a popular session player, moving back and forth between Los Angeles and Detroit. It was while living in Detroit that he recorded his famous solo on "Mercy Mercy Me (The

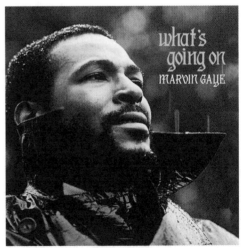

Gaye's masterpiece album, What's Going On, *almost never happened. Motown head Barry Gordy refused to release the title track believing it lacked commercial success. Gaye refused to record any new music until Gordy changed his mind.*

Photo © Photofest

these notes correctly and smoothly, practice the altissimo fingerings (given below the transcription) one at a time, making sure the pitches come out clearly and in tune. Then, slowly pick up the tempo until you can play along with the recording. Judging by the sound and phrases of this burnin' solo, it's no wonder why they call him Wild Bill!

Special Tips

Make sure to growl through the entire solo, really punch all the articulations, and make all the scoops wide. Also, don't forget to blow with a lot of air for a big sound.

Playing altissimo notes on the horn can be very difficult at first. My advice is to have a good, strong reed, use correct fingerings, and also experiment with different fingerings, as some work better than others on certain horns. Experiment with your embouchure and throat to help make the notes come out. Tightening your throat and/or pinching your lower lip on the reed helps, as does playing with an open, bright mouthpiece. Also try practicing some overtones on the saxophone, since the same embouchure and throat changes used for overtones are used to play altissimo notes. Finally, be sure to check out some instructional books on altissimo playing as well.

Ecology)." Bill Moore died on August 1, 1983 in Los Angeles.

How to Play It

Playing this famous solo requires pushing a lot of air into the horn to equal Moore's big tone. Using the growl technique throughout this solo will really give you that screaming sound that the song calls for. Furthermore, notice that all the scoops are really big and wide, and that hardly any vibrato is used.

Moore begins this solo beautifully by gradually expanding his melodic note range. In the first two measures, for instance, Moore hovers around the notes G and B. Then, in measures 3–4, he plays a line that reaches up a little higher to D. Finally, in measure 5, Moore leaps all the way up to a growling altissimo G, before

falling down into the palm key D. This kind of registral crescendo makes for a very satisfying opening to the solo. Another nice effect is the way Moore plays big scoops on his high B notes, which really gives measures 5–7 a lot of character.

The second half of the solo begins in measure 9 with some interval leaps that are rarely played on the horn. Particularly interesting is the low B♭ in measure 11 that quickly rolls up to the D, before arpeggiating a G minor triad over the static Cm9 harmony that holds for the remainder of the solo. Another nice detail is how Moore incorporates some sequential leaping intervals of a 3rd on beats 3 and 4 of measure 12.

The pickup to measure 14 and measure 15 contains the hardest part of the solo to play—we're talking some real altissimo high notes here! But of course Moore handles them with ease. In order to play

Vital Stats

Saxophonist: Wild Bill Moore

Song: "Mercy Mercy Me (The Ecology)"

Album: *What's Going On* – Marvin Gaye, 1971

Age at time of recording: 32

Saxophone: unknown

Mouthpiece: Brilhart Ebolin

Mercy Mercy Me (The Ecology)

Dick Parry

Pink Floyd is one of the most successful rock bands of all time, with timeless albums like *Dark Side of the Moon* and *The Wall*. The band, which formed in Cambridge and London in 1965, got its moniker by combining the names of two of their favorite blues musicians: Pink Anderson and Floyd Council. They released several albums in the late sixties and early seventies, but it wasn't until their 1973 masterpiece, *Dark Side of the Moon*, that they would make history and rocket to superstardom, selling over 40 million copies. The band also had other huge sellers with *Wish You Were Here* (1975) and *The Wall* (1979). Throughout the years, Pink Floyd has toured on and off with different lineups as its band members went solo, and at one time the various members fought over rights to use the band name. Today, Pink Floyd continues to sell millions of albums, and they remain a huge influence on musicians of all ages.

One of the most popular songs from *Dark Side of the Moon* is "Money," a unique and innovative song with a unique and innovative sax solo by Dick Parry. It remains the only song written in

Photo © Mick Hutson/Redferns

the time signature 7/4 to reach the top 20 in the U.S. It does switch to 4/4 during the guitar solo, since it was tricky to solo in such a strange meter for guitarist David Gilmour. Saxophonist Dick Parry sure doesn't have a problem with it!

Dick Parry was born on December 22, 1942 in Kentford, England. He was part of the band Joker's Wild in the mid sixties, and soon became a session player on various albums in the early 1970s. Being a childhood friend of Pink Floyd's David Gilmour, Parry also was persuaded to play on many of the band's studio albums. Memorable solos appear on "Us and Them" and "Money" (from *Dark Side of the Moon*), "Shine on You Crazy Diamond" (from *Wish You Were Here*), and "Wearing the Inside Out" (from *The Division Bell*). Parry also played and toured with Pink Floyd between 1972 and 2006.

He has also worked with John Entwistle and Rory Gallagher, and currently has been touring Europe with the Violent Femmes.

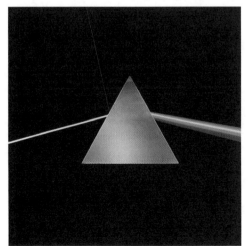

The album **Dark Side of the Moon,** *hailed as Pink Floyd's magnum opus, stayed on the Billboard charts for 741 consecutive weeks, the longest duration in music history.*

"We all like our music. That's the only driving force behind us. All the trappings of becoming vaguely successful—like being able to buy bigger amplifiers—none of that stuff is really important."
—Roger Waters of Pink Floyd

How to Play It

Dick Parry's solo on "Money" is wild, hypnotic, and innovative; he plays with a sound and style like no other! There was certainly some type of audio effect used on the saxophone to give it that semi-distorted sound. For the accompanying audio, I attempted to duplicate the sound of Parry's solo by offsetting two copies of my recorded version.

Your sound should be open and loud, and your embouchure should be somewhat sloppy. Imagine everything you're not supposed to do mouth-wise, and you'll have the sound (this isn't to say that Parry had a bad embouchure, but it's just what is needed here). Measure 1 starts with a flutter tongue on the G♯ with a long, gradual bend. In measures 3–4 there are a few key articulations to pay attention to. First, the C♯ is scooped at the beginning of measure 3, and is followed by a B that requires a fast vibrato. Finally the C♯ at the end of measure 4 should be played with the flutter tongue technique.

Parry starts the music in measure 5 on a screaming altissimo G♯ with shaky vibrato, similar to the way a guitarist would use the vibrato bar. (Articulate the notated rhythm in measure 5 by scooping the jaw, not by using the tongue.) In measures 6 and 7, the flutter tongue is added on the note E, and in measure 8, play the quarter notes with strong accents to underscore and lead into the chord change in measure 9. The trill in measure 9 (on the C♯) uses the side high E key throughout the measure. (Notice the octave note crack on the altissimo G♯ on beat 3. It's the cracked overtone, and I wonder if it was intentional or an accident?)

Photo © EMI Archives/Redferns

In measure 10, there's an interesting descending triplet pattern based on the C♯ minor pentatonic scale that should be articulated heavily. The rapid flurry of notes in the next measure is similarly based on the descending C♯ minor pentatonic scale, and is like a variation of the lick played in measure 10. Make sure to emphasize the bends on the C♯ notes at the end of measure 12, which leads us back to that wailing, flutter tongue G♯ in measure 13 (with the bend). Another overblown altissimo G♯ screams in measure 17, and should be played with a wide, jagged vibrato. In measure 18, Parry plays along with the band to fatten up the melody line before ending the sax solo with a rapid, aggressive trill on C♯ (using the high E key once again for the trill).

This smokin' solo is quite challenging to duplicate, especially without the use of the "distorted" sax sound produced on the Pink Floyd track. At first, it probably looks and sounds like no other sax solo you've ever heard. But practice it with the most outrageous sound and tone you can achieve and you'll have it!

Vital Stats

Saxophonist: Dick Parry

Song: "Money"

Album: *Dark Side of the Moon* – Pink Floyd, 1973

Age at time of recording: 31

Saxophone: King Super 20 Tenor

Mouthpiece: Otto Link (metal)

Words and Music by Roger Waters

David Sanborn

Photo provided by Frank Driggs Collection

"I have this sound in my head that I always try to get."
—David Sanborn

David Sanborn is the saxophonist who's launched a thousand tones! His soulful and screaming sax sound is arguably the most copied in music. He is admired not only for his session work (where he is responsible for some of the most famous sax solos in pop music), but also for the excellent solo albums he has released over the past 30 years. Sanborn's great solo on James Taylor's version of "How Sweet It Is (To Be Loved by You)" is just one of many we could have chosen for this book.

Singer/songwriter James Taylor was born March 12, 1948 in Boston, Massachusetts. He grew up in North Carolina where he started playing cello before switching to guitar around the age of 12. In 1968, Taylor signed with Apple Records in London, who released his debut album titled *James Taylor* later that same year. Poor album sales and drug addiction prompted Taylor's return to the United States, and it didn't take long before he was picked up by Warner Bros. Taylor's early acclaimed albums include *Sweet Baby James* (1970), *Mud Slide Slim and the Blue Horizon* (1971), *Gorilla* (1975), and his 1976 *Greatest Hits* album that has sold more than 11 million copies. In the wake of numerous GRAMMY® Awards, and being inducted into the Rock and Roll Hall of Fame in 2000, Taylor continues to tour and record today.

David Sanborn was born on July 30, 1945 in Tampa, Florida. He was diagnosed with polio as a child, and was urged by his doctor to take up a wind instrument in order to improve his breathing. Growing up in St. Louis, Sanborn was inspired by the R&B players and sounds he heard at the local clubs. He also cites Hank Crawford and members of the old Ray Charles band as major influences. Later, Sanborn studied at both Northwestern University and at the University of Iowa before joining the Paul Butterfield Blues Band, with whom he played at the original Woodstock.

Throughout the 1970s, David Sanborn became a sought-after session player, recording with artists such as David Bowie, Paul Simon, the Rolling Stones, and Stevie Wonder. In 1975, he released his first solo album *Taking Off*, and has since released over 20 solo records. He has been rewarded with six GRAMMYs®, and has sold eight gold records and one platinum. In the late 1980s, Sanborn was a regular guest-member of Paul Shaffer's band on "Late Night with David Letterman," and he co-hosted a late-night music show on NBC called "Night Music." Today, the "man with the sound" continues to record and tour, as well as influence and inspire countless saxophonists (like myself).

"How Sweet It Is (To Be Loved by You)" was originally recorded by Marvin Gaye in 1964, and reached #6 in the charts. Taylor's version rose all the way to #1 in 1975, making Sanborn's brief 8-bar solo a classic!

James Taylor's Gorilla *album features background vocals from David Crosby, Graham Nash, Valerie Carter, and his then wife Carly Simon.*

Photo provided by Frank Driggs Collection

and in measures 7–8, consult the fingerings given for the high F♯ and G♮. The solo ends by descending into almost an E blues scale, making this solo a classic Sanborn tour de force!

Special Tips

Try to play with an open mouthpiece (almost too open), and overblow into the horn hard to get an edgy, aggressive sound. Also, consider trying a metal mouthpiece (if you've ever played a metal Dukoff mouthpiece before, then you know where that bright, edgy tone comes from). Your embouchure should be really tight, and all the accents and articulations given in the transcription should be played heavily. Really lean into those bends, too!

How to Play It

Mix together a hard, bright tone with some note bends and wails and you'll have that famous Sanborn sound! Sanborn is one of those great players you can identify after hearing just two notes (unless it's one of those un-original Sanborn clones!).

The song has a shuffle feel, so make sure your eighth notes are played as quarter plus eighth-note triplets. Measure 1 starts with an accented G♯ and introduces some tight articulations that are used in the rest of the solo. In measure 2, the C♯ is overblown really hard, making the note have a harmonic split between the tones. The scooped G♮ in the same measure gives it all such a bluesy flavor. In measure 3, Sanborn plays a triplet pattern with a couple of the E notes almost "ghosted," making an aggressive, accented sound. In measure 4, we have once again that overblown Sanborn sound on the high C♯ notes, along with more bending of the G♮. In measure 5, make sure to use the forked E fingering,

Vital Stats

Saxophonist: David Sanborn

Song: "How Sweet It Is (To Be Loved by You)"

Album: *Gorilla* – James Taylor, 1975

Age at time of recording: 29

Saxophone: Selmer Mark VI Alto

Mouthpiece: Dukoff Super Power Chamber (metal)

How Sweet It Is (To Be Loved by You)

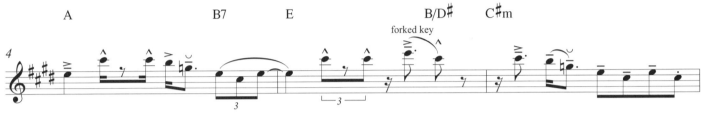

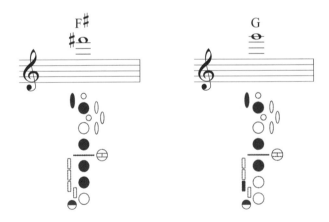

Words and Music by Edward Holland, Lamont Dozier and Brian Holland
© 1964 (Renewed 1992) JOBETE MUSIC CO., INC.
All Rights Controlled and Administered by EMI BLACKWOOD MUSIC INC. on behalf of STONE AGATE MUSIC (A Division of JOBETE MUSIC CO., INC.)
All Rights Reserved   International Copyright Secured   Used by Permission

Malcolm "Molly" Duncan

"Pick Up the Pieces" is one of those instrumental songs that everyone knows, and whenever it's played, everyone is up and dancing! This great, funky tune by the Average White Band is still covered regularly, and has become an R&B standard. The song is the result of a joint effort by all the members of the Average White Band. Each of the six original members grew up in Scotland listening to and playing music of American R&B, jazz, and Motown. Bassist Alan Gorrie, along with singer and guitarist Onnie McIntyre, led an R&B band called Forevermore while attending college. When Gorrie and McIntyre came together with a group of musicians (including sax player Malcolm "Molly" Duncan) for a session to record some original music, they quickly realized that they had created their own individual jazz-oriented soul. They modeled their sound on James Brown and Booker T. & the MG's,

The album AWB was originally rejected by MCA. After the band members crashed a party attended by Jerry Wexler and played him the album, he immediately signed the band to Atlantic Records.

and in 1972 (with the addition of some other players), decided to call themselves the Average White Band. The group performed all over Europe, including American military bases in Germany, and in several black clubs.

After appearing as the opening act for Eric Clapton's comeback concert at the Rainbow Theater in London, the Average White Band produced their first album, *Show Your Hand*, which was picked up by MCA Records. The band's unsuccessful American tour and poor album sales, however, caused MCA to soon drop them. Atlantic Records head Jerry Wexler nevertheless liked what he heard, and proceeded to sign the band, putting them in the studio with legendary arranger-producer extraordinaire Arif Mardin.

By the fall of 1974, the group's second album, *Average White Band*, was released. Amid several disco tracks, stood the true highlight of the album—the instrumental "Pick Up the Pieces." The song was first shunned by black stations because the band was white, but

support for the song from young listeners and DJs alike helped the band go #1 on the album and singles charts simultaneously in February 1975. In March of the same year, the song was a certified million-seller by the RIAA, and later was nominated for a GRAMMY® Award as Best R&B Instrumental. Later that summer, the Average White Band had another Top 10 hit with "Cut the Cake." But their happy success didn't last long with the tragic death of

"We wanted a vocal hook like James Brown used on 'Pass the Peas.' The group finally settled on 'Pick Up the Pieces.' "

—Owen McIntyre of the Average White Band

Photo provided by Frank Driggs Collection

drummer Robbie McIntosh, who died of a heroin overdose.

The band's later albums failed to reach the hit status of their earlier work, and they broke up in 1982, with members going on to play with artists such as Duran Duran and Paul McCartney. In 1989, original members Alan Gorrie, Owen McIntyre, and Roger Ball re-formed the Average White Band, and to this day the group continues to release albums and tour.

Malcolm "Molly" Duncan was born August 24, 1945 in Montrose, Scotland. Perhaps best known for his sax solo on "Pick Up the Pieces," he has also played with the Eurythmics, Ray Charles, Tom Petty, Buddy Guy, and Marvin Gaye. More recently, he released the album *Hornography* by Molly Duncan and the Frontline. Duncan currently lives in London and is actively performing throughout Europe. Meanwhile, "Pick

Up the Pieces" continues to be covered and used in movies and commercials, and remains one of the funkiest tunes ever written!

How to Play It

This solo by Duncan is so funky and great! Duncan starts with a nice note bend on the high E♭, making it sound real bluesy. Measure 3 has a C blues scale pattern, leading to a note fall on beat 1 of the next measure. Duncan plays some nice melodic lines that compliment the background horn hits perfectly in measures 5–13 on the original recording (not on the accompanying CD). In measure 6, the altissimo G comes from the forked fingering of the grace note F. In the next measure, Duncan seems to quote Nat Adderley's "Work Song," and

answers it in measure 8 with a bluesy-sounding gesture. Once again, make sure to use the forked fingering for the notes F and G in measure 9.

The most challenging part of the solo is the altissimo notes in measures 11–13. Duncan holds the altissimo C perfectly for six beats, before flawlessly going to the high D at the chord change. Practice this carefully as well as the altissimo notes from D to G in measure 13 to make sure those pitches are clean. Finally, Duncan ends the solo on a high note (pun intended) with a strong, scooped high G.

Special Tips

Practice the altissimo notes from C to D slowly making sure they both come out smoothly and in tune. The fingerings given below the transcription seemed to work best for me, although you may come up with other fingerings that suit you better. But be sure to always use the forked fingerings for E to F. Other than that, remember to blow really hard, stay in time (on top of the beat), and try to play with an edgy tone.

Vital Stats

Saxophonist: Malcolm "Molly" Duncan

Song: "Pick Up the Pieces"

Album: *Average White Band* – The Average White Band, 1975

Age at time of recording: 29

Saxophone: Selmer Mark VI Tenor

Mouthpiece: Otto Link NY #7 (metal) w/ Rico Jazz Select #3 or Van Doren Java 3 reeds

Words and Music by James Hamish Stuart, Alan Gorrie, Roger Ball, Robbie McIntosh, Owen McIntyre and Malcolm Duncan

Andrew Love

Courtesy of Minnesota Public Radio

"Takin' It to the Streets" by the Doobie Brothers is such a rockin' anthem piece! With the soulful singing of Michael McDonald over that bluesy gospel groove, all topped off with an incredible solo by sax legend Andrew Love—no wonder the song quickly became a timeless hit!

The Doobie Brothers (named after a slang term for marijuana) formed in San Jose, California in 1970. Their mixture of blues, country, and folk styles presented with a rock edge has made them one of the world's most popular rock bands. While the group's lineup may have changed over the years, their hits like "Listen to the Music," "Long Train Runnin'," "China Grove," "Takin' It to the Streets," and the GRAMMY® Award-winning "What a Fool Believes," still rock and sound great live or on record! The band continues to perform today with some of its original members.

Saxophone legend Andrew Love was born on November 21, 1942 in Memphis, Tennessee. His mother bought him his first tenor sax when he was 14. Love's earliest performances were of "Amazing Grace" at the Memphis Nebo Baptist Church, where his father was a pastor. Years later, while already doing sessions at Hi Records, Love was asked to play on sessions at the legendary Stax Records. It was at these sessions that he met trumpeter Wayne Jackson, and soon formed a musical collaboration that would become the renowned Memphis Horns. The Memphis Horns are likely the most famous and most recorded brass section of all time. Their signature sound can be heard on Aretha Franklin's "Respect," Otis Redding's "Dock of the Bay," and even on modern classics like Peter Gabriel's "Sledge Hammer" and Billy Joel's "River of Dreams."

Unfortunately, Love no longer plays today due to health reasons. The Memphis Horns currently have a CD/CD-ROM sample disc available that features them with their trademark sound. Even though they may have stopped recording together, Love and the Memphis Horns' tracks (and arrangements) are timeless and remain the epitome of horn-section playing!

How to Play It

Andrew Love's solo on "Takin' It to the Streets" is a perfect mixture of soul and funk that fits the song like a glove! Love's horn partner, Wayne Jackson, recalls that recording the solo, which occurred at Warner Bros. Studios in Studio City, California, "didn't take

Takin' It to the Streets *was the band's sixth studio album and the first to feature soulful singer Michael McDonald.*

"As far as I'm concerned, the Memphis Horns have been and still are the definitive soul horn section of my generation."

—Billy Joel

Photo provided by Frank Driggs Collection

more than one take. Andrew is extremely spontaneous and fast."

Measure 1 of the solo starts with a growl on the high D, which then goes into a quick fall on the B of beat 2 in the following measure. Measure 7 features a high F♯ (see the fingering below the transcription), and the upcoming measures use even more altissimo notes. In measure 9, a screaming high altissimo D is played while falling to the palm key D an octave below. Measure 11 is trickier, having the same altissimo D to D drop, but compressed within the span of two eighth notes. These two measures (9 and 11) are the most difficult of the

solo and should be practiced slowly. Notice that the solo uses a lot of high D notes, a pitch that happens to be the brightest and most open note on the horn. It's also one of the easiest notes to which you can add embellishments and articulations.

Special Tips

Practice the altissimo D until you get it in tune and sounding solid. Then try playing the measures with the octave falls slowly before speeding them up.

Also, make sure to play all the articulations precisely and heavily with a really open sound (by relaxing your jaw and embouchure), and play very aggressively!

Vital Stats

Saxophonist: Andrew Love

Song: "Takin' It to the Streets"

Album: *Takin' It to the Streets –* The Doobie Brothers, 1976

Age at time of recording: 35

Saxophone: King Super 20 Tenor

Mouthpiece: Berg Larsen

Takin' It to the Streets

Pete Christlieb

Steely Dan is often called one of music's most intellectual bands. Their crafty melodies and mixture of jazz harmony with rock and pop styles—not to mention their stunningly recorded studio albums (with the world's best musicians)—has made them one of the most successful and acclaimed rock/jazz bands.

The group was the creation of Donald Fagen (born January 10, 1948) and Walter Becker (born February 20, 1950) who met while attending New York's Bard College. The two started playing together as back-up musicians behind the pop act Jay and the Americans. As a songwriting team, Fagen and Becker were signed to ABC Records as staff writers, but weren't successful because their songs were considered too deep and sophisticated. The pair finally resolved to record for themselves, and formed a band. They got the name "Steely Dan" from a certain taboo object mentioned in the novel *Naked Lunch* by William Burroughs. The group's first album *Can't Buy a Thrill* was released in 1972.

The album Aja, with its jazz-influenced compositions, won the GRAMMY® Award for Best Engineered Non-Classical Recording in 1978.

It was with the album *Aja* that Steely Dan received the attention and respect they deserved, scoring hits with songs like "Peg," "Deacon Blues," and "Josie." The band's following album, *Gaucho*, was also a major success, but in its wake the creative duo ran out of steam and decided to take a break. Both founding members later pursued solo album projects—Fagen with *The Nightfly* (1982) and *Kamakiriad* (1993), and Becker with *11 Tracks of Whack* (1994).

In 2000, Steely Dan staged a comeback with the release of *Two Against Nature*, their first studio album in 20 years. The album won four GRAMMYs®, including one for Album of the Year. The band followed this success, releasing *Everything Must Go* in 2003. Today, Steely Dan continues to tour and record, thrilling old and new fans alike.

When Steely Dan wanted that stunning sax sound they heard on "The Tonight Show with Johnny Carson" every night, they called Pete Christlieb. In addition to performing with the Tonight Show Band, Christlieb carries the reputation of being one of the most successful and popular studio session players of all time. He has recorded with the likes of Count Basie, Benny Goodman, Quincy Jones, Sarah Vaughan, Chet Baker, and Woody Herman, to name a few. And who could forget his famous solo on Natalie Cole's hit remake of "Unforgettable"?

Christlieb was born February 16, 1945 in Los Angeles, California. He grew up in a musical family, with his father, Don, being a top-call studio bassoonist. Pete started on violin when he was six, but got interested in jazz and the tenor sax when he was 13. His first influences were Zoot Simms and Stan Getz.

Photo by Jos L. Knaepen

After playing with a variety of L.A.-based bands in the early 1960s, Christlieb joined drummer Louis Bellson's band in 1967, and continued to play with Bellson over the next three decades. Christlieb released his first solo album, *Jazz City*, in 1971. Working with Bellson then led to his gig with Doc

"I went in, they played me the track, I did a couple of takes, I was out of there!"

—Pete Christlieb (talking about recording "Deacon Blues")

Photo provided by Frank Driggs Collection

Severinsen on "The Tonight Show." Short snippets of Christlieb's burning solos were featured as the show came in and out of commercials (this is how Steely Dan first came to know and admire his playing).

In 1981, Christlieb started his own label, Bosco Records, which issued his albums as well as records by Bellson and composer/pianist Bob Florence. In addition to his activities playing with the Bill Holman Big Band and teaching during the summer months at the Bud Shank Jazz Workshop in Washington state, Christlieb continues to play on studio recordings for movies, television, and for other artists. Whenever anyone wants that perfect, soulful, melodic, jazz solo for their recording, they just call Pete!

How to Play It

Christlieb plays through this song's tough changes with such ease, that it's no wonder he's one of the greatest soloists out there! The solo is a perfect study in the use of melody, harmonic analysis, note bends, and the mixture of articulations. Each of Christlieb's melodic phrases could be a new tune itself!

The opening measures of the solo contain a beautifully refined melody line. Christlieb uses the side E♭ and D palm keys (no octave key) in measure 3 for openness and intonation. In measure 4, he presents a nice ascending rhythmic line that closes using the forked fingerings for E to F♯ over the bar line. The altissimo A and F♯ really pop out in measure 5, leading to the C♮ with a big scoop on it. Also notice that the lower A in measure 7 includes a rapid vibrato.

Measures 11–13 are the most interesting and difficult parts of the solo in terms of rhythm and fingering. Pete uses (I believe) the forked F♯ in measure 11. Where the G♮ is tied over into measure 12, Pete makes the difficult octave jump to high G sound easy. He continues in measure 12 with a descending pattern that is reminiscent of the famous "Cry Me a River" lick that many people use. To play it, use the forked G to F♮ fingering. Another challenging leap (a minor 9th) occurs later in the measure

from G♯ up to an altissimo A, before the solo line descends in measure 13 through the A blues scale (which again uses the side E♭ and D).

In measure 14, Christlieb throws in an interesting fingering for the second C♯ of beat 1; here he uses the overtone fingering for low C♯. To execute this, play the normal low C♯ fingering (with or without the octave key) and then get the overtone of the low C♯, which will sound an octave higher. In addition, make sure to play the C♯ at the end of measure 16 with a growl. Some nicely articulated intervals follow in measures 17–19. Make certain to emphasize the big scoops on the B notes in measure 20. In measure 21, Christlieb plays a great line that is repeated into the next measure before closing the solo with a descending A minor pentatonic scale stretched over measures 23–24 (ending with a side key D). Rhythmically, this phrase is so distinctive, and is a great way to dissipate all the energy that has built up over the preceding measures. As a whole, Christlieb's solo on "Deacon Blues" is absolutely amazing and just full of little gems rhythmically and harmonically! There are so many innovative ideas here to go with this truly difficult song!

Vital Stats

Saxophonist: Pete Christlieb

Song: "Deacon Blues"

Album: *Aja* – Steely Dan, 1977

Age at time of recording: 32

Saxophone: Selmer Mark VI Tenor

Mouthpiece: Berg Larsen (metal)

Phil Woods

Photo © David Redfern/Redferns

"I was in the middle of a meeting and 'Just the Way You Are' popped out of my head. I said, 'I gotta go home right now and write this song!'"

—Billy Joel

Billy Joel has definitely left his mark on pop music. With his selling over 100 million records worldwide, winning six GRAMMYs®, and continuing to pack concert venues everywhere, he's definitely one of the most successful pop singers in history!

Born William Martin Joel on May 9, 1949 in the Bronx, New York, Billy loved classical music at an early age, and began taking piano lessons. Years later, he took up boxing and made his way on the amateur Golden Gloves circuit (before quitting after having his nose badly broken). In 1973, Joel signed with Columbia Records, and his first album, *Piano Man*, was a huge success. Even greater success came with his 1977 album *The Stranger*, with the track "Just the Way You Are" going on to become Joel's first U.S. Top 10 single (#3) and subsequently winning GRAMMYs® for both Song and Record of the Year. Joel composed the song as a birthday gift for his first wife, but vowed after they divorced to never perform it again.

Joel would later score #1 hits like "It's Still Rock and Roll to Me," "Tell Her About It," and "We Didn't Start the Fire," and pen other classics like "Piano Man," "My Life," and "Uptown Girl." In 1987, he became the first American pop star to play the former U.S.S.R. After some musical and personal ups and downs over the years, Joel recorded *Fantasies and Delusions* in 2000, which featured his own classical compositions. He later embarked on a world tour with singer Elton John, breaking stadium attendance records everywhere. Today, Joel continues to tour and record, and recently has had success with the Broadway musical *Moving Out*, which features many of his classic songs. He was also inducted into the Rock and Roll Hall of Fame in 1999, and is currently the sixth best-selling artist in the U.S. And despite Joel's vow never again to perform "Just the Way You Are," the song has become a pop and jazz standard round the world, having been recorded by more than 100 artists. Joel's timeless version of the song features a sax solo by jazz legend Phil Woods.

Phil Wells Woods was born on November 2, 1931 in Springfield, Massachusetts. He picked up the alto sax in his early teens, and soon fell under the influence of greats like Benny Carter and Charlie Parker. Woods moved to New York and attended Juilliard (as a clarinet major) and the Manhattan School of Music. He made a name for himself by attending jam sessions, playing with the Charlie Barnet Big Band, and playing many recording sessions. He went on to play with such musical giants as Quincy Jones, Dizzy Gillespie, Buddy Rich, and Benny Goodman. Today, Woods continues to record and tour with his own popular jazz groups. He has received several GRAMMY® Awards and continues to inspire players as one of the greatest alto saxophonists of all time.

Generally regarded as Joel's best work, The Stranger *remains his best-selling non-compilation album to date, selling over ten million copies.*

Photo provided by Frank Driggs Collection

How to Play It

Solo 1

Phil Woods adds some jazz flavor to this bossa nova–style pop song with his classic sax solo. To begin the solo, Woods plays three measures of the song intro before going into his actual solo. Measure 4 is actually almost a solo break before the solo begins at measure 5. Make sure that all the low B to F♯ notes in measures 1–3 sound smooth and clean (not blasted). Notice his use of a wide vibrato on the E and the F♯ notes to finish each melody line of the first three measures. Woods also uses interesting combinations of articulations throughout the solo. Measure 8, for example, contains scoops on the G♯ notes, where measure 9 starts a nice melody with a new articulation that continues into measures 10–11. In these same measures, Woods weaves beautiful lines around the chord tones of the backing harmony. In measure 12, the G♮ on beat 3 nicely adds the ♭13 to the B7 chord. Woods continues outlining the song's chord changes in measures 13–14 with his beautiful sound.

Measures 15–16 initiate quite a rhythmic departure with quarter-note triplets, and the ascending stepwise line really builds the tension as it leads up to the A♯ in measure 17. Also note that Woods plays the final triplet in measure 16 using the "doodle tongue" on the notes D♯, F♯, and G♯. Doodle tonguing is when you quickly touch and leave your tongue back on the reed after the initial tonguing, giving the notes a darker timbre. This articulation is very common in jazz playing, and it adds an interesting color to a line. The tension from the A♯ remains in measure 17 when Woods lands on the dissonant G♮, which is a tritone away from the root of the accompanying C♯7 chord. In measures 18–19, Woods pushes the tension level even higher, as his solo line climbs upward using another interesting articulation in which he tongues every two notes. This ascent leads to the high E in measure 19, after which Woods lands once again on a note (C♮) that is a tritone away from the root of the backing F♯7 chord. He ends perfectly with a descending line, ending on the 5th note of the B chord.

This great solo alone would have been enough, but you can never have too much Phil Woods.

Solo 2

Phil Woods's second solo starts at the big key change of the song. The opening line in measure 1 sort of sounds like a quote from "The Christmas Song," but then Phil unleashes a serious bebop jazz pattern in measures 5–6. Notice the rapid, jazz articulation that he plays on this double-time lick over what turns out to be an excellent iv–V–I pattern (Em7–F♯7–B). Woods throws in a tasteful bend in measure 6 on the first note of beat 2 that should be laid back.

The song goes back to its original key in measure 7, with Woods playing a soulful, high D♯ with light vibrato. The original recording of the song starts to fade out gradually around measure 9. It's still audible enough to hear Woods throw in another doodle tongue on the D notes of beats 2 and 3 in measure 9. In measures 17–18 there is a lot of long, tenuto tonguing on a melodic line based on the B major pentatonic scale. As the original recording really starts to become inaudible, try to listen closely for the end of the solo. Note: The song version represented here ends at measure 21 (there is a longer version in which the fade is audibly longer).

Special Tips

Exaggerate the various articulations used in this solo, keep your fingers relaxed, and aim for a relaxed tone. Also, pay special attention to playing the solo in time (especially on the killer sixteenth-note passage in measure 5 of solo 2).

Vital Stats

Saxophonist: Phil Woods

Song: "Just the Way You Are"

Album: *The Stranger –* Billy Joel, 1977

Age at time of recording: 45

Saxophone: Selmer Mark VI Alto

Mouthpiece: New York Meyer (hard rubber)

Just the Way You Are

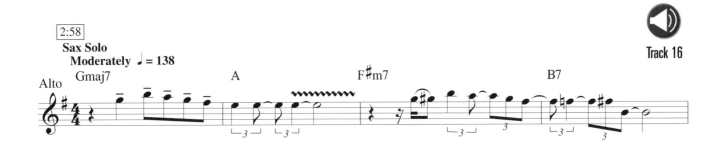

John Helliwell

Photo © Fin Costello/Redferns

"I went into a small studio bathroom with my sax, head- phones, and some magazines to keep me occupied between takes."

—John Helliwell (on recording "The Logical Song")

The group Supertramp is one of the most successful rock bands to come out of England in the past 30 years. They got their name from W.H. Davies's book *The Autobiography of a Super-Tramp* (pub. 1908). The band was signed to A&M Records with their LP *Crime of the Century* going #1 in the U.K. But it wasn't until their sixth album, *Breakfast in America* (1979) that they really hit the big time. The record made it all the way to #1 worldwide with hit singles like "Take the Long Way Home," "Goodbye Stranger," and "The Logical Song"; as of today, it has sold more than 18 million copies worldwide.

Their hit "The Logical Song" reached #6 on the U.S. charts. The band recorded several takes of the song, and according to saxophonist John Helliwell, "it was recorded live with no overdubs, and fortunately they chose the one with the good sax solo." Helliwell also confirms the rumor that he did indeed record his solo in the studio bathroom, due to the lack of recording booths available.

Supertramp went on to record other hits like "Give a Little Bit," "It's Raining Again," and "My Kind of Lady." Lead singer Roger Hodgson left the band in 1983 to pursue a solo career, leading to the group's breakup in the late 1980s. A few members of the band re-formed Supertramp in 1997, and they continue to tour and release albums.

John Anthony Helliwell was born on February 15, 1945 in Todmorden, West Yorkshire, England. He came from a musical family and was surrounded by music at a young age. He started with piano and recorder lessons before a family friend's jazz records inspired him to take up the clarinet at age 13. Helliwell joined the Todmorden Symphony Orchestra while barely a teenager, and by age 15 he bought his first alto saxophone. Soon, he was playing in several school groups, and he became heavily influenced by jazz players like Cannonball Adderley, Sonny Rollins, Miles Davis, and Art Blakey. He took a job as a computer programmer, yet music always remained important to him.

In August 1973, John received a call from Dougie Thomson asking if he was interested in joining the band Supertramp. He took the job and recorded the album, *Crime of the Century*, which became a hit record in the U.K. Helliwell recorded and toured with the band all the way up to the 1990s when the band went on hiatus. At that time, he moved back to England to study at the

Supertramp's Breakfast in America, *along with selling over 18 million copies worldwide, won GRAMMY®s for Best Recording Package and Best Engineered Album Non-Classical in 1980.*

Photo © GAB Archives/Redferns

Royal Northern College of Music in Manchester, and later ended up joining forces once again with ex-Supertramp singer Roger Hodgson. Today, John lives in London and plays with his band, John Helliwell's Creme Anglaise, which performs a mixture of jazz, funk, blues, soul, and rock.

How to Play It

Solo 1

This song features two different solos by Helliwell. Considering the way the chords are accented during the first solo, I believe the meter changes between 4/4 and 2/4 in the form (notated in the solo). Either way, Helliwell handles the changes and their rhythms with ease!

Some items to pay attention to at the beginning of the first solo include the glissando from E to high E♭ with a growl in measure 1, and the bend on E♭ (using the "y'all" jaw movement) in measure 2. In measure 3, use the side D key to play the "turn" ornament on beat 3.

The first beat of measure 5 has another note turn going to high D, which you can play while leaving your finger down on the C key. Measures 6–7 repeat a blues lick that really accents the E♭s. Practice the altissimo A at the end of measure 9 (the fingering is given beneath the transcription) and the glissando fall down to the G in measure 10. Notice that the first nine measures of the solo are based on the A blues scale. Measures 12–13 contain another repeating blues lick based on the one employed in measure 6. The E♭ notes are accented, adding tension and concluding a perfect rock saxophone solo by Helliwell.

Solo 2

Obviously one Helliwell solo just wasn't enough, so a second one appears at the end of the song until the track fades out. The second solo starts off with a bang, as a big growl adds bite to more accented E♭ notes alternating with D. Measure 5 has some very short staccato notes leading to jaw-drop scoops on the E♭ notes of the following measure. The lick in measure 10 is basically a trill between E and G terminating with a note slide up to (and then down from) the A in measure 11. Also, the two A notes in measure 12 should have big bends on them, with the second one being quite short.

Measure 14 contains a line embellished with ascending trills using the right-hand high E key (à la Cannonball Adderley). In measure 16, Helliwell plays a descending blues lick derived from the one he played in measure 6 of the song's first solo. Notice the quick fall between the C and A sixteenth notes as well (measure 16, beat 3). Also, don't miss the articulation variations that Helliwell plays in measures 19–21. The record starts fading out around measure 20, but you can still hear that the trill is once again played using the right-hand side E key in measures 23–24.

In "The Logical Song," Helliwell created a classic solo for a classic song. When asked if he was thinking of any particular concept for the solo, John replied that he was "thinking of Cannonball Adderley." By the look and sound of it, you can certainly sense the influence!

Vital Stats

Saxophonist: John Helliwell

Song: "The Logical Song"

Album: *Breakfast in America* – Supertramp, 1979

Age at time of recording: 33

Saxophone: Selmer Mark VI Alto

Mouthpiece: New York Meyer 7 (hard rubber) or Selmer Soloist: E (hard rubber)

The Logical Song

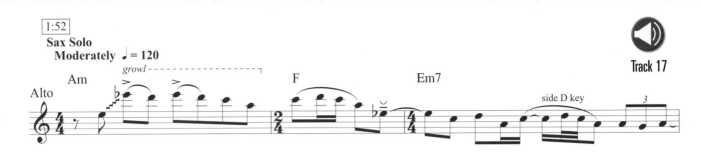

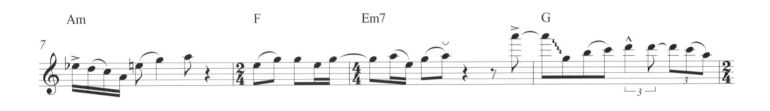

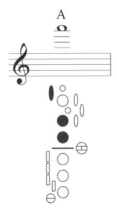

Don Myrick

Photo provided by Frank Driggs Collection

"After the Love Has Gone" by Earth, Wind & Fire is a timeless love song that is still very popular today. This great song also happens to feature a smokin', soulful sax solo by R&B legend Don Myrick.

Earth, Wind & Fire is easily one of the greatest R&B/pop/soul bands ever, having sold over 40 million albums in the U.S. alone. The group was founded in 1969 in Chicago by Maurice White, who put together the band's name from its members' astrological signs. Over the years, they perfected an amazing mixture of funk, jazz, soul, pop, gospel, and African music, and their lavish live shows filled with special effects were not something to be missed!

"Shining Star" was Earth, Wind & Fire's first hit, going #1 on both the pop and R&B charts in 1975; the song later won a GRAMMY® for Best R&B Vocal Performance. Maurice and the gang also had hits like "Reasons," "Sing a Song," "Let's Groove," and 1979's GRAMMY®-winning "After the Love Has Gone" (which reached #2 on the pop and R&B charts). The band decided to take a break in the mid 1980s, with lead singer Philip Bailey going on to have a successful solo career.

Today, with a total of six GRAMMYs® and an induction into the Rock and Roll Hall of Fame in 2000, Earth, Wind & Fire continues to tour and record with members of the original band.

Saxophonist Don Myrick was born April 6, 1940. During the late 1960s and early 1970s he and Maurice White were both members of a Chicago-based jazz/funk group called the Pharaohs. From the Pharaohs, Myrick became the leader of the world famous Phoenix Horns, who would later become Earth, Wind & Fire's original horn section.

Myrick was also a successful session player, and appeared on numerous albums including organist Jack McDuff's *The Heatin' System* and pianist Ramsey Lewis's *Goddess Sun*. In addition to his memorable sax work on such Earth, Wind & Fire classics as "After the Love Has Gone" and "Reasons," Myrick is also best known for his playing with Phil Collins, particularly on the hit "One More Night." Tragically, Don Myrick was shot and killed by the officers of the Los Angeles Police Department in a case of mistaken identity on July 30th, 1993.

> *"What's happening with me and a lot of other people who made good records is that we understood composition. We had an appreciation for the music we were influenced by, but at the same time, we were able to put our own identification on it."*
>
> —Maurice White, founding member of Earth, Wind & Fire

The album I Am *may have been Earth, Wind & Fire's answer to the disco era with their single "Boogie Wonderland," which also won a GRAMMY® along with "After the Love Has Gone."*

Photo © Photofest

rarely find in a pop song (or in a pop ballad for that matter). But Myrick sure makes it work!

As the recording begins to fade out at measure 18, we can still hear Myrick laying down some electrifying bebop jazz lines in measures 20–21. By measures 22–24, however, the rapid note flurries become increasingly difficult to hear (and notate), yet I have tried to transcribe them as best as possible (more "sheets of sound"). There is so much we can learn from Don Myrick in this amazing solo, including the fact that you can add a bit of traditional jazz flavor to a pop song—and with amazing results!

Special Tips

This solo uses a great variety of articulations, including the jazz articulation. Try playing all the written articulations with a jazz sound, and make sure to play the sixteenth-note lines in time. As in learning any new song, start slowly and work conscientiously; soon you will be playing right along with the original recording.

How to Play It

If you weren't sure whether or not Don Myrick could play bebop jazz, this solo should prove it to you! With its mixture of a big sound, bebop jazz lines, and wailing, soulful notes, Myrick's cookin' solo is flawless and inspirational.

I just love the first four measures of this solo. What an opening! Make sure to play the glissando in measure 4 between the D and F in the triplet figure. Measures 5–7 contain a ii–V–I progression (B♭m7–E♭7–A♭maj7) with a great solo pattern that you should practice in all 12 keys!

Measures 9–11 contain some serious bebop sixteenth-note lines that Myrick plays perfectly in time, and with a jazz articulation. In measures 13–15, the ii–V–I pattern reappears, and Myrick's rapid solo lines almost turn into "sheets of sound" à la John Coltrane. Notice in particular the fall between the D♭ and B♭ in measure 13; I wonder if it was intentional or simply a slip of the finger? Measures 17–21 feature more double-time bebop lines, the likes of which we

Grover Washington, Jr.

Saxophone great Grover Washington, Jr. is almost single-handedly responsible for the explosion of smooth jazz in the 1980s and 1990s. With classic instrumental hits like "Mister Magic," "Black Frost," "Winelight," and the R&B classic "Just the Two of Us," Washington is one of the most influential and successful saxophone players in modern jazz history (Kenny G should send some royalty checks his way!).

Born December 12, 1943 in Buffalo, New York, Grover grew up around music with his dad being a sax player, and his mother a church chorister. His dad gave him his own sax at age ten, and by 12 he was playing professionally. Grover performed with a group called the Four Clefs from 1959 to 1963, at which time he was drafted into the U.S. Army. While in the army, he met up with drummer Billy Cobham, who would later introduce him to many players in New York. Washington spent a few years in New York after the army, but he eventually settled in

GROVER WASHINGTON, JR.
WINELIGHT

CONTAINS "JUST THE TWO OF US" WINNER OF TWO GRAMMY AWARDS

Winelight became a best-selling album for Washington on the strength of radio-friendly "Just the Two of Us," which was the only non-instrumental song on the album.

Philadelphia. After subbing for R&B legend Hank Crawford on a recording session, Washington was offered a record deal with Motown Records who released his first album, *Inner City Blues*, in 1971. It was his fifth album, *Mister Magic* (1974), that brought Washington commercial success, due in large part to the popularity of the title track (which has since become an R&B standard).

With the success of his following albums, he became a major headliner, selling out concerts halls and dazzling audiences by playing all the saxes (alto, tenor, soprano, and baritone). *Winelight*, his 1980 album for Elektra Records, would become his biggest seller due to its smash hit single "Just the Two of Us." The track featured vocals by soul artist Bill Withers, and it would go on to win a GRAMMY® Award for Best R&B Song of 1981; the album *Winelight* was also awarded the GRAMMY® for Best Jazz Fusion Performance.

Grover Washington, Jr.'s huge sound, jazzy melodic riffs, and soulful playing would influence many saxophone players throughout the 1980s—including Kenny G, Najee, George Howard, and Boney James—and basically marked the beginning of the smooth jazz genre (be it

Photo provided by Frank Driggs Collection

"I don't think in categories. My job is to explore and express music of the heart."
—Grover Washington, Jr.

good or bad). In addition to making his own records, he also produced three albums for the Philly band Pieces of a Dream. Washington's popularity even took him to the White House, where he

Photo © Echoes Archives/Redferns

Grover Washington, Jr.'s soul/jazz-influenced melody lines and horn mastery on "Just the Two of Us" are all over this classic track. Notice that his tone has a dark and full roundness to it that obviously comes from a hard rubber mouthpiece, not metal. Play this solo with a big, full sound, and keep your embouchure very open and loose.

The solo actually enters on the last two measures of the repeating four-bar vamp. Washington starts the solo on a low C that resolves quickly into the D chord tone. The first seven notes of the solo create a motif that Grover will revisit several times throughout the solo (which sounds similar to the background vocal line). To make sure that the initial low C doesn't "pop" out too loudly, approach it softly like Grover does, and be sure to add that fast and jagged vibrato on the low D as well. The entire opening gesture over the first three measures of the solo is based on the G blues scale (including the C♯ grace note), and the accents on beats 2 and 3 of measure 1 highlight the rhythmic groove that the band is establishing, so be sure to hit those pretty hard.

In measure 2, Grover plays his motif again, but notice here how it works against a different set of chords than at the beginning of the solo. Again, try not to "pop" the low C too hard. As a whole, measures 2–5 consist of another G blues lick that is basically a variation of the solo's opening three measures. Take note of Grover's wide vibrato on beat 3 of measure 4, and really make the written articulations crisp and tight in measures 5 and 6, which will make the line more effective. Also, scoop the B♭ in beat 1 of measure 6 before going back down the now-familiar motif that stretches from beat 3 of measure 6 through beat 2 of measure 7. Articulate the C♯ in measure 7

had the honor of performing for President Bill Clinton's 1993 inaugural celebration.

Sadly, on December 17, 1999, Washington suffered a fatal heart attack after taping a segment for the CBS "Saturday Early Show" in New York. He was 56 years old. In March 2000, Sony Classical released Washington's final recording project, an album of classical opera arias aptly titled *Aria*. Through his recordings, the legacy of Grover Washington, Jr. lives on as he continues to inspire up and coming jazz artists and music fans of all ages.

How to Play It

The first thing to know about the classic song "Just the Two of Us" is that there are two main versions out there: the album version and the radio edit single. It is the radio single (featuring a shorter sax solo) that is the best-known version of the song, and it remains a staple on the airwaves to this day. The solo presented here comes from that single.

by bending your jaw in a tight and then loose position to make the pitch bend up, then down.

On beat 4 of measure 7, Grover plays a B♭ major pentatonic scale descending in sixteenth-note triplets all the way down to the low B♭ on beat 1, measure 8. Make sure to play all the notes of measure 8 with a long, legato articulation, and pay attention to the scoop on the D of beat 4; this will set up the groove by putting heavy accents on the downbeats. Measures 9–10 also feature heavy articulations, and are once again based on the G blues scale. After playing the C♯ grace note, you'll want to scoop the high D tied over into measure 10, and then scoop the following B♭ as well.

Measures 11 and 12 are the hardest measures in the solo. Bend the C♯ at the beginning of the measure, and play the following triplet sixteenth notes smoothly, evenly, and in time. The two triplet figures on beats 3 and 4 are basically just note "turns" (if it helps to think of them that way). Practice each one slowly and gradually increase your speed until you are playing up to tempo. Also, use the side C key when playing the turn on beat 4. Measure 12 has another note turn on beat 3, which you should

play using the side D key instead of your regular D fingering. This fingering will be easier, faster, and cleaner. Leading from measure 12 into measure 13, we encounter the recurring motif again, although it's compressed rhythmically at the beginning. After you play the altissimo G in measure 13, use the forked F key to play the following F. Also, scoop the palm key D again on beat 2 of measure 14, and use your side D key again for the turn on beat 2 of measure

15. Grover plays his motif one last time leading from measure 16 into measure 17, which goes into a high altissimo G just as it did back in measure 13. As the song fades out, leave your finger down on the C while using the palm key D on the turn of measure 18, beat 3.

As you can now see and hear, this great solo from a great song has some serious jazz-oriented lines, as Grover clearly shows his roots.

Vital Stats

Saxophonist: Grover Washington, Jr.

Song: "Just the Two of Us"

Album: *Winelight* – Grover Washington, Jr., 1980

Age at time of recording: 37

Saxophone: H. Couf Gold-plated Tenor

Mouthpiece: Berg Larsen (hard rubber, 130/0)

Photo by David Redfern/Redferns

Just the Two of Us

Words and Music by Ralph MacDonald, William Salter and Bill Withers

Junior Walker

When the rock band Foreigner needed something burnin' for their song "Urgent," they knew Junior Walker was just the man to give it to them. Well, they asked for it, and they got it! Junior's solo on "Urgent" is probably the most insane, guitar-like solo to ever appear on a pop record. And man is it hard to duplicate!

The band Foreigner has definitely left its mark on rock and pop music, selling more than 50 million records worldwide. The group got its name from the fact that the six original members were drawn from either side of the Atlantic (three from Britain and three from America). Guitarist Mick Jones took charge in assembling the group in New York City in 1976, and soon they were signed to Atlantic Records in 1977. Jones also formed a strong songwriting partnership with lead singer Lou Gramm, and the two soon collaborated on early hits like "Feels Like the First Time" and "Cold as Ice." Their self-titled debut album has sold more than five million copies, and their follow-up album, *Double Vision*, has sold over 7 million, with its popular cuts

Photo by Avenue Pictures Productions/Photofest

Foreigner's **Four** *album would sell over six million records thanks to hit singles "Urgent," "Juke Box Hero," and the classic power ballad "I Want to Know What Love Is."*

"Double Vision" and "Hot Blooded" reaching #2 and #3, respectively, on the U.S. charts. Other hits followed, including "Urgent" (#4 U.S. and #45 U.K.), "Waiting for a Girl Like You" (#2 U.S. and #8 U.K.) and the 1984 #1 U.S. and U.K. smash "I Want to Know What Love Is."

By the time Foreigner recorded their fourth album in 1981, there were only four members left in the band, so it's only logical that they would call the album *4*. The switch from being a sextet to a quartet also meant that the band would turn to session players to augment their sound. Fortunately they found Junior Walker to tear it up as the guest soloist on "Urgent." The success and popularity of Walker's distinctive solo led him to later record his own version of the Foreigner hit.

"I was blowing like [Illinois Jacquet], trying to do some things like him. And that's where I got it from. I started blowing that high note. Then I just went on up a little higher than what he was doing."

—Junior Walker

Photo © Photofest

Despite their success, tension between Jones and Gramm reached a peak in the late 1980s, with Gramm eventually leaving the band. Both artists would go on to release solo albums before reuniting for a "hits" album in 1992. Reunited, Jones and Gramm weathered hard together until 2003, when Gramm left the band once again for a solo career. Meanwhile, Foreigner continues to tour today, with Jones as the only original member.

For Junior Walker's bio, see "Shot Gun."

How to Play It

Prepare to play a solo like no other! This one recorded by Walker was spliced together from several different takes. For the most part, the solo is based on the F# minor pentatonic scale and features some of Walker's trademark R&B playing. Included are some screaming altissimo notes that would raise anyone's eyebrows!

Right from the start, the solo hits us with some screaming high notes! I believe Junior plays these first three high notes by getting the super-high overtones as he fingers lower notes. For example, the altissimo C# is played using the low C# fingering, the altissimo E is played using the low C fingering, and the double altissimo F# is played using the low B fingering. You really have to overblow the horn (almost making it sound like a squeak) to get such high overtones, and you also have to play the quick fingering changes. In addition to playing the high notes, you'll need to work on your growl and flutter tongue techniques as well. The C# notes in measure 2, for example, should be articulated with wide scoops and a growl, while the C# notes in measures 3–4 require the flutter tongue. Also make sure to accent the eighth notes in the second half of measure 4 very heavily. Another great place where Junior uses the growl is on the lick that begins at the end of measure 5 and goes to the beginning of measure 7.

In measure 9, Junior uses the flutter tongue again on the long C#, and in measures 12–15, he wails out the highest tenor sax notes I've ever heard played on a recording! These screaming altissimo notes are again most likely played by using the higher overtones of lower notes; the double altissimo G# is played using the low C# fingering and the double altissimo F# is played using the low B fingering. In measure 16, Walker comes down from those high notes with a descending F# minor arpeggio that he articulates heavily and with a growl.

Special Tips

In order to play the overtone altissimo notes, make sure to have a strong reed, an open, bright mouthpiece, and experiment with other fingerings that may make the notes come out. Being able to play overtones on the sax is a very important technique for reaching altissimo notes and for tone development. Consult a good technique book for information on how to play overtones, or better yet, find a good teacher who can properly demonstrate and explain how to play them. Once you do that, practice! Playing overtones is difficult at first, but they are a *must* for playing altissimo high notes.

Vital Stats

Saxophonist: Junior Walker

Song: "Urgent"

Album: *4* – Foreigner, 1981

Age at time of recording: 50

Saxophone: Selmer Mark VI Tenor

Mouthpiece: Lawton (metal)

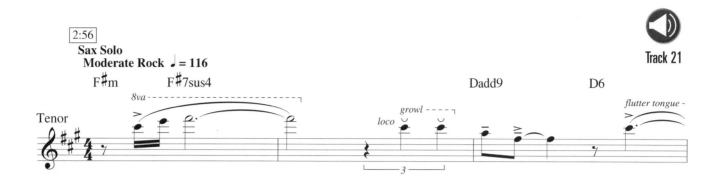

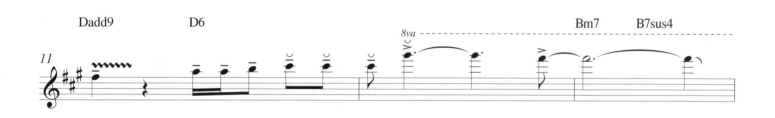

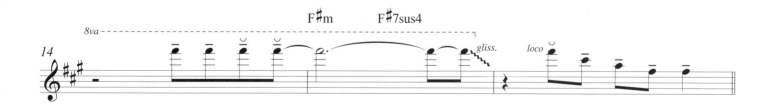

Words and Music by Mick Jones

Sonny Rollins

Photo © David Redfern/Redferns

"I know I can play me, but I want to play something that fits into what this is about."

—Sonny Rollins (talking about recording with the Rolling Stones)

Sonny Rollins is responsible for some of the greatest sax solos in the history of music. His mastery of improvisation has allowed him to become one of the most innovative tenor saxophonists the jazz world has ever seen. Check out any of his solo records and you'll be blown away! It's no wonder why this jazz master continues to influence saxophone players throughout the world, and it's no wonder why the Rolling Stones wanted Rollins to play on their record.

The Rolling Stones definitely live up to the name "the world's greatest rock band," selling more than 240 million records worldwide. Founding members Brian Jones, Mick Jagger, and Keith Richards were heavily influenced by American blues and R&B performers, and in 1962 they named their band after the Muddy Waters song "Rolling Stone." The Stones were always considered the bad boys of rock 'n' roll, opposite their fellow countrymen, the Beatles. In 1964,

Photo © Photofest

ballads like "Start Me Up," and "Waiting on a Friend." The album stayed at #1 for nine weeks. In the decades that followed, the Rolling Stones would increase their superstar status by releasing more hit albums like *Voodoo Lounge* (1994) and their incredibly popular greatest hits collection, *Forty Licks* (2002). Today, the band continues to mount massive world tours, and has become renowned for selling out record numbers of concerts. They easily remain one of music's greatest bands!

Sonny Rollins was born Theodore Walter Rollins on September 7, 1930 in New York City. He studied piano at an early age and began the alto saxophone at age 11. It was when he was 16 that Rollins (inspired by Coleman Hawkins) found his voice on the tenor. Some of Rollins's neighborhood friends included musicians Jackie McLean, Arthur Taylor, and Kenny Drew. He went on to record and perform with Charlie Parker, Bud Powell, Thelonious Monk, and Miles Davis—all before he was age 20! It was in the mid 1950s that Rollins finally arrived, winning *Down Beat* magazine's prestigious critics poll as the "new star" of the tenor saxophone. Around this time he also acquired the nickname "Newk"

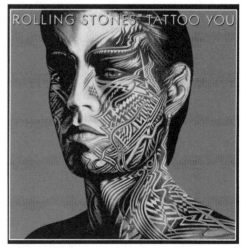

Tattoo You is composed of outtakes—including some songs that date back a decade earlier—with new overdubs and vocals added. "Waiting on a Friend" is one such song, with recording beginning around 1972 and finally released in 1981.

they had their first American Top 40 hit with "Tell Me (You're Coming Back)," followed by others like "Time Is On My Side," "The Last Time," "Jumpin' Jack Flash," and their biggest hit, "(I Can't Get No) Satisfaction," which stayed at #1 on the charts for four weeks in 1965.

So far, the band has released over 40 albums, with their songs reflecting such changing musical fashions as the psychedelic craze and disco. In 1981, the Stones once again scored big with the release of their album *Tattoo You*, which featured a mix of rock 'n' roll hits and due to his striking resemblance to Brooklyn Dodgers pitcher Don Newcombe. Rollins later became a member of the Clifford Brown/Max Roach Quintet, and soon was recording for both Prestige and Blue Note Records. Some of his famous recordings include *Newk's Time, Saxophone Colossus, The Bridge, Way Out West*, and *A Night at the Village Vanguard* (Volumes 1 and 2). Rollins was one of the first musicians to turn popular show tunes into jazz standards, and he pioneered the piano-less tenor saxophone trio.

Due to personal and musical frustrations, Rollins withdrew from music between 1959 and late 1961. When he returned, he began to experiment with the avant-garde free jazz movement of the 1960s. From 1969 through 1971 Rollins once again took a hiatus from music, but since his return in 1972, Rollins has continued to perform and record, gaining worldwide acknowledgment as the greatest living jazz soloist.

How to Play It

Solo 1

What Rollins displays in this great solo is that you don't have to be flashy by playing a lot of fast or high notes. On the contrary, here it's all about rhythm, melody, and the variety of articulations that makes the solo great!

Most of Rollins's solo is based on the D major pentatonic scale, and features an alternation of tenuto and staccato tonguing. Use the palm keys to play the high E notes in measures 1–3, and use the forked E to F♯ fingering for those particular pitches in measure 7. In measures 9–11, Sonny shows us an elegant lick that climbs up the D major pentatonic scale from its 5th (A) and exhibits an amazing mixture of articulations and rhythms. In measures 13–14, he throws in a fantastic glissando that flies from a low D all the way up two octaves before settling back down an octave on the middle D (all played with a growl!). Make sure to play all written articulations and use the growl where noted.

Solo 2

The second solo is a continuation of the ideas Rollins presents in the first; its lines are again very melodic and heavily articulated. In measures 3–4, he plays some big bends on the B and high E, all while growling. In measures 5–9, Rollins uses a very wide vibrato with a growl, and sustains the high D quite awhile, taking a breath only in measure 6 where the eighth-note rest is notated. Measure 10 has probably the biggest bend I've ever heard, and it adds such an emotional quality to the solo! To play it, drop your jaw down as far as you can without letting the note break, and then bend the note back up. The farther and wider you can bend it, the better!

Measures 11–12 highlight a Rollins trademark—jagged, offbeat rhythmic patterns—which terminates with another glissando from high D to middle D in measure 13. More rhythmic fluctuations come in measures 20–25, as Rollins decorates a repeating pattern of alternating 3rds supporting the G6 and Dadd9 chords of the song. To be more specific, notice in measure 20 how the first beat features a descending 3rd from B to G, while the beginning of measure 21 features a descending 3rd from A to F♯; Rollins continues this pattern, oscillating between B–G and A–F♯ on the downbeats of measures 22–25. In measures 25–29, Rollins switches to a variation of his repeating pattern, and in doing so, shifts the focus to the end of each measure. Notice that the last beat of each measure now fits into an alternating pattern between A and G (or later, A–G and G–F♯). As the record begins to fade near measure 26, the closing measures of the solo become increasingly inaudible until the end.

It's truly amazing the way Sonny Rollins's heartfelt sax work on "Waiting on a Friend" communicates the song's poignancy with musical notes. In his two solos, he also shows that a true master improviser can play in any style, over any groove, and make it sound magnificent.

Vital Stats

Saxophonist: Sonny Rollins

Song: "Waiting on a Friend"

Album: *Tattoo You –* The Rolling Stones, 1981

Age at time of recording: 51

Saxophone: Selmer Mark VI Tenor

Mouthpiece: Lawton (metal)

Words and Music by Mick Jagger and Keith Richards

Steve Norman

The song "True" by the eighties sensation Spandau Ballet has become another one of those romantic songs that are timeless. Once the band's biggest hit, today it can still be heard in commercials, movies, and on television. The song also features a simple, memorable sax solo by band member Steve Norman.

Spandau Ballet was one of the most commercially successful new wave groups of the early 1980s. The band emerged from London's underground club scene in the late seventies and pioneered a sound combining synthpop and funk. They are often associated with the "New Romantic" movement in music and fashion, which emphasized flamboyance and glamour, as opposed to the nihilistic anti-fashion of the punk scene. Spandau Ballet's enormous popularity as a club band led to their eventual signing with Chrysalis Records. They released several albums that sold very well in Britain, but it wasn't until their third album, *True*, that they would become international superstars.

Released in 1983, *True* reached #1 on the U.K. album charts and #19 in America. The success of the album is credited to the title track, which became the standout hit reaching #1 in the U.K. and #4 in the U.S. The band released several more albums later in the 1980s, eventually shifting toward more of a rock sound, but their albums failed to do much in the U.S. despite being successful elsewhere. The band broke up in 1989, which would mark the beginning of a series of bitter lawsuits over royalties that would carry on into the 1990s. Recently the band has reformed for a reunion tour, minus lead singer Tony Hadley, who originally sang all the band's biggest hits.

Band member Steve Norman was born on March 25, 1960 in London, England. He started out as a guitarist for Spandau Ballet, and eventually added saxophone, percussion, and other instruments. He even composed the song "Motivator" for their 1989 album *Heart Like a Sky*. Steve is responsible for the memorable sax solos on other Spandau Ballet songs like "Through the Barricade," "Gold," and "I'll Fly for You."

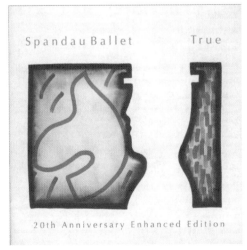

Spandau Ballet — True

20th Anniversary Enhanced Edition

The timeless title track would go on to be sampled on PM Dawn's "Set Adrift on Memory Bliss," Nelly's "N Dey Say," and still continues to show up in movies and commercials.

"The Christmas before last I bought myself a sax. I convinced the other lot I could play it, so they got me a better one. It's just something I'm good at— learning to play instruments."

—Steve Norman (speaking in 1983)

After playing with Spandau Ballet, Steve got married and moved to the popular resort island of Ibiza, where he formed the band Cloudfish. He has written and produced for the Italian female group Quintessenza, and also writes for the magazine *Ibiza Now*. Steve is also part of the Spandau Ballet reunion band that is currently on tour.

How to Play It

One unusual aspect about the sax solo on "True" is that it happens over the song's bridge. Another unusual aspect is Steve Norman's tone, which is hard to duplicate, because it's nearly the opposite of what we usually strive for on the sax—a hard, open, and focused sound (typically produced with a metal mouthpiece on the tenor). Norman's tone, however, is almost reminiscent of a high school sax student, but in a good way because it's a romantic sound that fits the song perfectly. At the time of the recording, Norman had not yet been playing the sax a long time. It's a great pop solo that many people have asked about over the years.

In measures 1–3, the solo begins with the nice melody built from the first five notes of the F major scale. The lick in measure 4 outlines a descending F triad (C–A–F), but decorates each of the main pitches with the note that sits above it in the scale; this fits nicely over the B♭add9

Photo provided by Frank Driggs Collection

chord. Going into measure 6, play the high notes using the palm keys E and F (without fork), and play the whole phrase (to measure 7) very legato. Measure 9 starts with a glissando up to the A, before going into a sharply articulated melody line through measure 11.

To play the pickup notes into measure 13 and the high F, use the palm keys again, and be sure to add vibrato to the high F. Also, remember to take a big breath in measure 12 so that you'll be able to play all the way through the final flourish of sixteenth notes (all slurred) that descend down to the final E in measures 15–16.

Finally, take notice of all the scoops and bends that Norman plays, and try playing with a softer, less-focused sound.

Vital Stats

Saxophonist: Steve Norman

Song: "True"

Album: *True* – Spandau Ballet, 1983

Age at time of recording: 22

Saxophone: unknown

Mouthpiece: unknown

Track 24

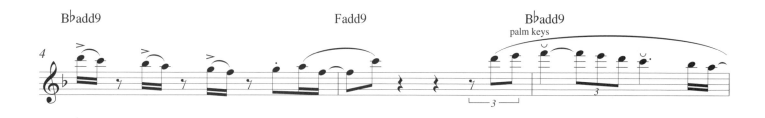

Words and Music by Gary Kemp

Charlie DeChant

Photo courtesy of Sheila DeChant

"The studio had a digital delay without much memory, so I had to record the solo thinking that it was to be repeated four beats later."

—Charlie DeChant (talking about recording "Maneater")

The song "Maneater" is one of the many hits recorded by Daryl Hall and John Oates, the most commercially successful rock duo in pop music history with six #1 singles and a total of 19 gold and platinum albums. Daryl Hall (born October 11, 1946) and John Oates (born April 7, 1949) first met in 1967 while attending Temple University in Philadelphia. As the story goes, the two ducked into a freight elevator to escape a riot that had erupted during a battle of the bands gig at the Adelphi Ballroom. After that fateful introduction, the pair realized they had similar musical tastes and ambitions, so they decided to start a band. Hall & Oates signed with Atlantic Records in 1972, but it wasn't until moving to RCA that they would enjoy their first Top 10 hit with "Sara Smile" (1975) and their first #1 single with "Rich Girl" (1976).

In 1980, Hall & Oates scored their next of many #1 hits with "Kiss on My List," from the album *Voices*, followed by "Private Eyes," and "I Can't Go for That (No Can Do)" from their 1981 album *Private Eyes*. The duo's seventh LP, *H2O*, remains their most successful record to date, having reached #3 on the album charts. It spawned three Top 10 singles, including the #1 single "Maneater," which would go on to become the biggest hit of their careers (staying at #1 for four weeks and selling over two million copies). They had other hits like "Say It Isn't So" and "Out of Touch" (#1 in U.S.).

In the late 1980s, Hall & Oates signed with Arista Records, yet failed to have the commercial success they enjoyed in the past. In 2003, they were voted into the Songwriter's Hall of Fame, and many of their classic songs continue to be covered and sampled by artists. Today, Hall & Oates continue to tour and record together, and have secured their place as one of the most successful songwriting duos of all time.

Hall & Oates sax man Charlie "Mr. Casual" DeChant was born in Long Beach, California in 1945. He grew up in Pennsylvania and Florida, and started playing the alto sax in the school marching band; at 16, he received a tenor for his birthday. DeChant credits Stan Getz and Paul Desmond as his first influences (later he got into David "Fathead" Newman, Charlie Parker, and John Coltrane). He played in various bands in obscure clubs around Florida, and eventually took some music courses at Florida International University and at the University of Miami. DeChant joined the pop duo Hall & Oates in the late 1970s, and has been with them ever since.

DeChant is an extremely versatile musician, playing all the saxes, the flute, the keyboard, and the guitar, as well as being a composer. Besides playing and touring with Hall & Oates, he has performed and recorded with the bands Plan 9, Bethlehem Asylum, and on various other albums, including Daryl Hall's solo records. In addition, DeChant has released two solo albums of his own, *The Moon at Noon* (1996) and *Like the Weather* (2006), featuring all original tunes.

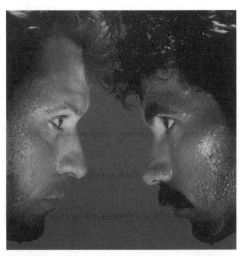

H2O was the duo's biggest-selling album, sparking three Top 10 singles: "Family Man," "One on One," and the monster #1 hit "Maneater."

How to Play It

Charlie DeChant's great solos have been featured on several Hall & Oates hits like "I Can't Go for That (No Can Do)" and "One on One," but his solo on "Maneater" takes the cake! It features a great "call and response" solo played with a digital delay. As DeChant recalls, "the digital delay at Electric Lady Studios in New York didn't have much memory, and the idea was to have the sax repeated. So I had to record the solo thinking that it was to be repeated four beats later. It [the delay] was later added in the mix."

The solo begins on a single pitch, C#, gradually expanding every other measure until we get the first four notes of the C#

minor scale in measure 7 (talk about building a solo from the ground up!). DeChant's methodical and deliberate expansion at the beginning of solo really builds the tension and heightens our expectations as both the number of notes and the register of each gesture increases.

Notice that the line in measures 7 and 10–11 use a typical jazz articulation, and that the high notes in measures 13–14 use the palm keys for E. Measure 17 again involves the palm E, and this passage up through measure 19 is also played with a growl. The "off-beat" rhythms in measures 21–22 offer a nice bit of variety (especially with the delay effect) before the repeating pitch pattern (C#–D#–E) finally pushes up to the climax of the solo on the high F# in measure 23. Notice that this completed

line (C#–D#–E–F#) is the same motif DeChant worked his way up to in measure 7. Pretty ingenious, don't you think? Measures 25–27 should be played with the growl, which makes the solo sound more aggressive toward the end. Also notice that the palm E key is used (instead of the forked E) in measures 27 and 31–32.

Charlie DeChant's solo on "Maneater" is so perfect with the digital delay giving it that mysterious, "played on the street" vibe. It's also a great example of how to build a solo by starting out with a simple idea, then building it up, and finally ending big, yet leaving listeners wanting more. What more could you ask for in a solo?

Special Tips

Make sure to play with the growl in the right spots, use the palm key E in the right places, and try to get a full, open sound. The brighter the better!

Vital Stats

Saxophonist: Charlie "Mr. Casual" DeChant

Song: "Maneater"

Album: *H2O* – Hall & Oates, 1983

Age at time of recording: 37

Saxophone: Selmer Mark VII Tenor

Mouthpiece: Otto Link (metal)

Words by Sara Allen, Daryl Hall and John Oates
Music by Daryl Hall and John Oates
Copyright © 1982 by Unichappell Music Inc., Hot Cha Music Co. and Geomantic Music
All Rights for Hot Cha Music Co. Administered by Unichappell Music Inc.
All Rights for Geomantic Music Controlled and Administered by Irving Music, Inc.
International Copyright Secured   All Rights Reserved

V. Jeffrey Smith

Simply put, V. Jeffrey Smith is one talented man! He is an accomplished producer and vocalist, he plays guitar, bass, drums, keyboards, and flute, and his sax solos have graced some of the most popular songs of the 1980s. With several solos to choose from, it's Smith's solo on Billy Ocean's "Caribbean Queen (No More Love on the Run)" that remains his most famous.

Vernon Jeffrey Smith was born on February 25, 1954 in Harlem, New York. By the age of nine, he taught himself how to play the guitar as well as a number of other instruments; he learned to play the saxophone in junior high school at age 13. While in college, Smith studied with the great Yusef Lateef and played with saxophonist Frank Foster, all while keeping busy playing weddings, bars, funerals, and "even a few orgies" (according to Smith himself!).

Suddenly was the album that made Ocean an international star, staying on the charts for over a year and a half. It hosted three pop hits: "Loverboy," "Suddenly," and "Caribbean Queen (No More Love on the Run)."

As a producer and performer, Smith has worked with artists such as Whitney Houston, Daryl Hall, Stevie Wonder, Paula Abdul, Des'ree (producing her #1 hit, "You Gotta Be"), Heather Headly, and Tamia. But it was his saxophone solos on cuts like Billy Ocean's "Get Outta My Dreams, Get into My Car," "When the Going Gets Tough, the Tough Get Going," and "Caribbean Queen" (and on Debbie Gibson's "Only in My Dreams" and "Foolish Beat") that Smith would leave his indelible stamp on pop music history. Although he was approached by major record labels to pursue a solo career, Smith passed. In his own words, "My dumb, radical butt passed on all of it. But I don't regret it."

"When I went into the booth, I just started playing to find the key and familiarize myself with the format of the song."

—V. Jeffrey Smith (talking about recording "Caribbean Queen")

It was Smith's solo on "Caribbean Queen (No More Love on the Run)" that marked his introduction to the airwaves. According to Smith, "When I went into the booth, I just started playing to find the key and familiarize myself with the format of the song. The whole time I was playing, the great producer Keith Diamond had the foresight to have the tape rolling from the very beginning. So I played through the whole song and when the song finished I said, 'Let's try it.' But he said, 'Come in the booth.' I thought maybe I was gonna get the boot, but he said, 'I think we got what we need.' We took parts from different parts of the song and constructed what would be a classic! One of the first lessons I learned about producing, and one that I use to this day in my productions: *always keep the tape rollin'*—because magic can happen on a first take."

In 1988, Smith formed the group the Family Stand with partner Peter Lord and singer extraordinaire Sandra St. Victor. They have released four albums on Atlantic/Elektra Records, and have accumulated a massive cult following worldwide with their intense live performances and poignant thumping sound. They had a hit in the early 1990s with the song "Ghetto Heaven."

Today, Smith resides in Brooklyn, New York where he owns his own studio, Phantom Power Productions and has just finished a new Family Stand album titled *Super Sol Nova, Vol. 1*, which was released independently in early 2007 in Europe. Check out www.thefamilystand.net and www.myspace.com/thefamilystand for more information on the band.

How to Play It

V. Jeffrey Smith's solo on "Caribbean Queen" remains an incredibly hot, singable, and memorable solo. So memorable in fact that Smith says he's consistently approached by musically inclined fans who can hum the solo for him note-for-note—sure proof of a classic! This 16-bar solo says so much that it's basically a new song in itself. Smith starts off with a soulful, accented altissimo G and A in measure 1, using the palm keys for the E to F on beat 3. He repeats the same figure two measures later, making it a "call and response" phrase. In measures 6–7, play the bend on the F♯ with the "y'all" jaw movement. The rhythm pattern beginning in measure 9 most likely uses the alternate "1 and 1" fingering for A♯ on the grace notes, which gives both the bend and the grace note a more effective bend in pitch. Smith repeats the lick in measure 11, but ends it differently in measure 12 as he leaps up to E with an overdubbed harmony part added a 3rd above. Measure 13 has a bend on the altissimo B♭ (again using the "y'all" jaw movement) going into an altissimo A–G followed by an E that you should play using the palm key. Smith's solo ends with a descending E minor pentatonic scale (using all legato tonguing) before a final glissando rips from B up to another palm key E.

Photo © Photofest

Vital Stats

Saxophonist: V. Jeffrey Smith

Song: "Caribbean Queen (No More Love on the Run)"

Album: *Suddenly* – Billy Ocean, 1984

Age at time of recording: 30

Saxophone: Selmer Mark VI Tenor

Mouthpiece: Dukoff S10 (metal) w/ Rico Royal 3.5 reeds

Kenny G

Photo by Ken Settle

"It's important to let each artist do what makes him or her feel comfortable. Success should be a by-product of that."
—Kenny G

Kenny G may be the most famous saxophonist in the history of the instrument. And with over 75 million record sales, he's the biggest-selling instrumental musician of all time. This great solo of his appears on Smokey Robinson's "One Heartbeat."

William "Smokey" Robinson was born February 19, 1940 in Detroit, Michigan. He acquired the nickname "Smokey Joe" as a child because of his love for cowboy movies. In his teenage years, Robinson sang in a popular band that eventually renamed itself the Miracles. In the late 1950s, Robinson developed a close relationship with songwriter/producer Berry Gordy and encouraged him to launch his own record label, which became Motown Records. The Miracles were one of the first groups signed to the label and Smokey became a leading figure in the organization, serving as the company's vice-president from the years 1961–1988.

In their first decade, Smokey and the Miracles had major hits with songs like "Shop Around," "Ooo Baby Baby," "I Second That Emotion," and "The Tears of a Clown" (#1 in the U.S. and U.K). As a composer, Robinson had success writing hits for other Motown artists, penning classics like "My Guy," "My Girl," "Get Ready," and "The Way You Do the Things You Do." In 1965 the band was officially renamed Smokey Robinson and the Miracles.

Smokey became a solo artist in 1971 and has continued to write and record hits like "Baby That's Backatcha," "Cruisin'," "Being with You," "Just to See Her," and "One Heartbeat" (#3 pop, #10 R&B). He still records and tours today, and recently launched a line of frozen soul food. In total, Smokey has over 4000 songs to his credit. Truly amazing!

Kenny G (Kenneth Gorelick) was born June 5, 1956 in Seattle, Washington. He first fell in love with the saxophone after seeing a sax player on "The Ed Sullivan Show." Soon thereafter, Kenny took up playing the alto, with Grover Washington, Jr. being one of his first influences. In 1976, Kenny played his first professional job with the Barry White Love Unlimited Orchestra. After graduating with an accounting degree from the University of Washington, Kenny landed the gig playing with the Jeff Lorber Fusion and recorded on their 1980 album, *Wizard Island*. As a result of playing with Lorber, Kenny was offered a solo artist contract from Arista Records in 1981. Although his albums were commercially successful from the start, it was his fourth album, *Duotones* (1986), which made him a star. The record's single, "Songbird," went to #4 on the pop charts, with the album eventually selling over five million copies.

After *Duotones*, Kenny's recording career flourished with the release of hugely successful albums such as *Silhouette*, *Kenny G Live*, *Breathless* (featuring the GRAMMY®-winning song "Forever in Love"), and *Miracles*. He also became a sought-after session player for artists like Toni Braxton, Babyface, Whitney Houston, Michael Bolton, Johnny Gill, and, of course, Smokey Robinson. At present, Kenny G continues to tour and maintains a thriving recording career, adding more accolades every year. He may just be the most widely known saxophonist in the history of the instrument!

One Heartbeat *was Smokey's 39th album (including albums with the Miracles). His amazing career has spanned an astonishing five decades.*

How to Play It

Of all the great Kenny G solos to choose from, his brief alto sax solo on Smokey Robinson's "One Heartbeat" is quintessential! Here, we find Kenny doing what he does best—playing flawless notes and melodies that fit the song perfectly!

From the beginning of the song, Kenny incorporates little sax fills to tease us with a taste of what's to come for the solo. When the solo does arrive, Kenny eases into it by quoting the same melody he has already established throughout the song. After that, he lets loose, unleashing his magic touch! Play the first note, B, with a gradual crescendo and with vibrato. Notice how Kenny uses such a fast vibrato on all the notes that are at least a half note in value. Most of the solo sticks around the B major pentatonic scale, within which Kenny crafts some very interesting melodic lines. Notice the large leap (a minor 7th) that Kenny plays between measures 4 and 5 to the long altissimo B. As with the other long notes in this solo, be sure to play this one with a fast, tight vibrato. In measure 6, the solo line cascades down from the altissimo B in a pattern that is embellished with note "turns." This descending pattern emphasizes the root and 5th of the B major scale (B and F♯), which appear alternately on each beat in the measure. Finally, pay close attention to the D♯–E–D♯ turn on beat 3 of measure 7. It requires a fingering that is tricky to play quickly, so make sure you practice this and play it in time.

Photo provided by Frank Driggs Collection

Special Tips

The hardest part of the solo occurs in measure 5, where you must play the long B followed by the note turns in the next measure. Practice these altissimo notes and fingerings slowly and cleanly, and make sure they're in tune.

Vital Stats

Saxophonist: Kenny G

Song: "One Heartbeat"

Album: *One Heartbeat –* Smokey Robinson, 1987

Age at time of recording: 30

Saxophone: Selmer Mark VI Alto

Mouthpiece: Beechler (hard rubber)

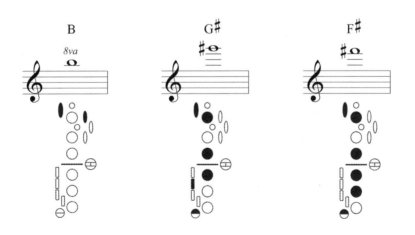

Gary Herbig

If you've never heard Gary Herbig, then you don't watch movies or TV. Gary is definitely one of the most frequently-recorded and widely-heard saxophonists of the last 30 years. Ever wonder who plays the clarinet on the theme from "Cheers," or who's responsible for that wailing solo on Donna Summer's "She Works Hard for the Money," or who's really behind the sax solos in the *Police Academy* movies? Well, it's Gary!

Gary Herbig was born May 7, 1947 in Missoula, Montana. He attended the University of Montana from 1966–69 on a clarinet scholarship. After graduating, he moved to Los Angeles and began studying sax with the legendary Bill Green. Practicing ten hours a day paid off, as he quickly became one the busiest session players in town.

As a studio session player, Herbig recorded TV theme songs for shows like "Alf," "Rosanne," "Home Improvement," "The New Dating Game," and "Three's Company." And some of his famous pop solos appear on Rod Stewart's "Some Guys Have All the Luck," Donna Summer's "Bad Girls," and "She's Like the Wind" from the *Dirty Dancing* soundtrack. Herbig even did two tours with Elvis! In the late 1980s, Herbig released two solo albums, *Gary Herbig* and *Friends to Lovers*, reaching the top ten on the Billboard contemporary jazz charts. And did I mention that he played the Montreal Jazz Festival opposite Miles Davis? To continue listing all of Gary Herbig's amazing film, TV, and album credits would require a book of its own!

Today, Gary keeps busy doing studio session work, writing, teaching free master classes, and revisiting his roots in Montana. He recently released the CD *Montana Shooting Star*, and remains an extremely friendly and inspirational person with a big heart!

Due to the huge commercial success of the Dirty Dancing *soundtrack (over 11 million sold), a second album,* More Dirty Dancing, *was soon released, selling over four million units.*

> *"Baseball players bat .300 and make millions. Studio musicians have to bat a thousand all the time, or we don't work!"*
> —Gary Herbig

How to Play It

Gary Herbig's solo on the song "(I've Had) The Time of My Life" is only eight bars long, yet what a marvelous eight bars they are! The song, which was composed by Franke Previte and sung by Bill Medley and Jennifer Warnes for the movie *Dirty Dancing*, went on to win the Oscar® for Best Original Song in 1987. It also happened to be the very *last* song the makers of the film pulled from a box of demos that had been submitted for the movie. We're certainly glad they chose it, and we're especially glad that Gary ended up playing the solo!

Photo © Echoes Archives/Redferns

Photo by Bill Greenblatt/Getty Images

This short 8-bar solo typifies the way sax solos traditionally work on pop records—you get eight bars to tell a story, and then you get out. Luckily, in eight bars Gary can tell volumes! The solo bursts right out the gate with a long, soulful high F♯ that falls beautifully into a nice melodic lick in measures 2–3. Measure 4 features a rapid guitar-like descending pattern, with the F♯ notes providing a nice bit of color as the 9th of the accompanying E chord. In measure 5, Herbig jumps to an altissimo G♯ and F♯ before descending into an F♯ bluesy lick (like in measure 2). The chromatic line in measure 7 adds another nice bluesy touch, before approaching the hardest notes of the solo,

which are the pickup notes to measure 8. The ease with which Herbig plays the altissimo A–G♯–F♯ is amazing, so making these three notes clean and resonant may take some practice. Gary ends the solo with a descending lick based on an F♯ blues pattern.

This solo is certainly one of the finest to ever grace a pop song, and it simply couldn't have been done better. The control, soulfulness, and mastery that Gary has on the horn is truly inspirational.

Vital Stats

Saxophonist: Gary Herbig

Song: "(I've Had) The Time of My Life"

Album: *Dirty Dancing* soundtrack – various artists, 1987

Age at time of recording: 39

Saxophone: Selmer Mark VI Tenor

Mouthpiece: Dukoff S10S (metal)

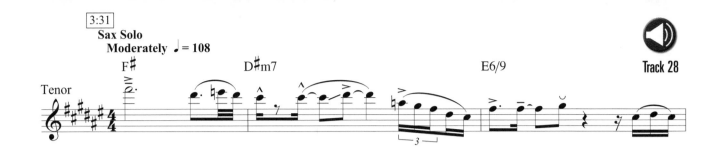

Sax Solo
Moderately ♩ = 108

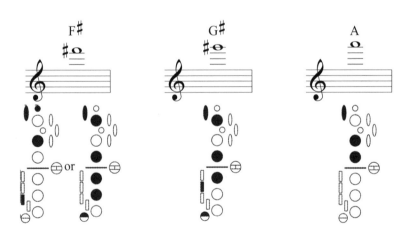

Candy Dulfer

Photo provided by Frank Driggs Collection

After the pop success of Saxuality, *Dulfer would go on to sell more solo records in the smooth jazz genre.*

Candy Dulfer is turning into one of the leading "voices" of modern saxophone. With her critical success as a solo artist, as well as her work with Prince, she's definitely on her way to becoming a voice that will be around for a long time. Born September 19, 1969 in a small village near Amsterdam, she began playing the soprano sax at age six. Her father, Hans Dulfer (a successful tenor sax player himself) gave Candy lessons and exposed her to the music of jazz greats like Sonny Rollins, Dexter Gordon, Coleman Hawkins, and Charlie Parker (who became her favorite). Candy Dulfer made her professional debut at age 11, and played at the North Sea Jazz Festival at age 12. She formed her own band at age 14, but passed on several record deal offers as a solo artist (until 1990, when she signed with BMG).

Candy's band, Funky Stuff, gained wide popularity in the Netherlands after opening for Madonna in Rotterdam in 1987. Two years later, the band was scheduled to open for Prince, but those shows were suddenly cancelled. Dulfer eventually did end up playing for Prince, and went on to perform on his *Graffiti Bridge* soundtrack. Since then, she and Prince have maintained a strong music relationship and have collaborated and toured together.

Another major artist who would change Candy's life was ex-Eurythmics member Dave A. Stewart. After hearing a demo of hers, Stewart invited Candy to record some tracks for a Dutch movie he was scoring called *De Kassière* (known in English as *Lily Was Here*). Candy recorded the title track, "Lily Was Here," in one take, thinking it was nothing. To her amazement, the song was released as a single four months later and shot to #1 in Holland, England, and Europe. The incredible success of the single prompted Stewart to share its royalties with Candy on account of her presence and improvisation on the track. The song also appears on Dulfer's first solo album *Saxuality*.

Since then, Candy Dulfer has worked with such popular music greats as Patti Labelle, Aretha Franklin, Van Morrison, the Time, Maceo Parker, and Pink Floyd. She has sold a total of three million units worldwide with hit albums like *Saxuality*, *Sax-A-Go-Go*, and *Right in My Soul*, and most recently was on tour with Prince.

> *"I recorded my part in five minutes. I was hoping they wouldn't put it on the album. I was so embarrassed. It was so simple and I even played off-key. It wasn't until later that I learned to appreciate it and saw what a genius Dave Stewart is."*
>
> —Candy Dulfer (talking about recording "Lily Was Here")

Photo © BBC Photo Library/Redferns

How to Play It

Candy Dulfer is known for playing some mean and funky R&B/smooth jazz sax, and this solo shows it! Her sound is similar to that of David Sanborn, but not as edgy and bright. The solo is in the more difficult key of C♯ minor, yet she handles it with ease.

The first two pickup measures of Dulfer's solo begin with a strongly thematic descending idea that, like most of the solo, is based on the C♯ blues scale (note the prominence of the G♮ "blue note"). There is certainly a seamless, organic quality to Dulfer's lines, and this continues as the solo progresses.

Measures 7–8 consists of an ascending C♯ blues scale played with heavy accents that ends on the 9th of the C♯ minor chord, adding a nice splash of tonal color. Notice how Dulfer plays her C♯ blues scale lines in measures 10–12 with a jazz articulation. In measures 13–14, she takes these ideas further by incorporating some very inventive and effective bebop runs. In measures 15–16, the solo returns to a more blues-oriented style as the heavily-accented eighth notes climb up the blues scale to C♯, setting up the next chorus.

The repeated B notes in measure 17 add a pleasant harmonic richness as they supply the flat 7th to the backing C♯ minor chord. Similarly, the A♯ in measure 17 really brightens the tonal palette as it evokes the C♯ Dorian mode. From measure 19 to the end, Dulfer's solo again leans heavily on the C♯ blues scale. Notice in measures 20–21, amidst the flurry of sixteenth notes, how Dulfer restates the lick she played at the beginning of measure 11. The only difference is that now she displaces the pattern so that it begins on beat 3 (instead of beat 1), causing the lick to extend over the bar line. In measures 21–22, Dulfer incorporates some nice rhythmic variations as she plays an ascending E pentatonic scale (starting on the 3rd, G♯). Play this passage with long, legato tonguing. The solo ends perfectly with some heavily-accented C♯ notes, starting with quarter notes and then accelerating to eighth notes.

In examining this solo, we can see what a great job Dulfer does in mixing and connecting different melodic lines in ways you might not normally think of, taking the listener on a wonderful journey of twists and turns. In addition, Dulfer uses all the styles and elements that make a great timeless solo: blues, bebop jazz, various articulations, and inventive melodic phrases that really tell a story!

Special Tips

Getting the right tone for this solo requires backing off the air and pinching your embouchure (yet you still want an edgy tone). Use a lot of heavy, aggressive tonguing, and make sure to learn the C♯ blues scale and have it under your fingers. Finally, play all the sixteenth notes evenly and in time, while using the correct jazz articulation.

Vital Stats

Saxophonist: Candy Dulfer

Song: "Lily Was Here"

Album: *De Kassière (Lily Was Here)* soundtrack – Dave Stewart, 1989; *Saxuality* – Candy Dulfer, 1990

Age at time of recording: 19

Saxophone: Selmer Mark VI Alto

Mouthpiece: Saxworks (metal) w/ Rico Jazz Select #3 medium filed reeds

Conclusion

So there you have it, 25 of the most famous and significant sax solos of the 20th century! These classic solos are something to cherish, as the future of the 8-bar sax solo looks dim. In my opinion, with the unfortunate decline of quality pop music and the emphasis on the visuals or images of music rather than the actual music itself, the "sweetener" saxophone solo seems like a thing of the past. (I can't think of one hit song recently that includes a sax solo!) Let's hope that someday the music will make a full circle for the best, and not only return to the catchy, timeless pop, rock, or R&B songs, but bring back that wailing sound of a great sax solo as well (even for eight bars). Until then, we'll always have these classics!

About the Author

Eric J. Morones hails from Racine, WI. He attended the University of Wisconsin-Whitewater, where he received a degree in Communications and a minor in Music. He also attended the University of North Texas where he worked on a Master's Degree in Jazz Studies. Eric currently lives in Los Angeles where he has played, toured, and/or recorded with the Brian Setzer Orchestra, Bobby Caldwell, Steve Tyrell, Maureen McGovern, Jack Sheldon, Bill Holman, Chad Wackerman, and Will Kennedy. His sax playing is featured on the Big Fish Audio Sample DVD *Suite Grooves*. He has performed at the Montreux and North Sea Jazz Festivals, as well as on "The Tonight Show with Jay Leno," "Late Night with Conan O'Brien," "Jimmy Kimmel Live!," "The Today Show," "FOX Channel," "Live with Regis and Kelly," and Woodstock '99.

As a writer, Eric wrote a bi-monthly column for the *Saxophone Journal* called "From the Front Lines," and produced two master-class CDs for the magazine, "How to Play Pop, R&B, and Smooth Jazz" and "How to Play the Blues." He also wrote the books *101 Saxophone Tips* and *Paul Desmond Saxophone Signature Licks* (both Hal Leonard Publishing). Eric's first solo jazz CD *About Time!* is released on Arabesque Records.

Today, he continues to play in various groups around L.A., teaches private lessons, records for various films and artists, and keeps busy with many music-related projects.

www.ericmorones.com

ARTIST TRANSCRIPTIONS®

Artist Transcriptions are authentic, note-for-note transcriptions of today's hottest artists in jazz, pop and rock. These outstanding, accurate arrangements are in an easy-to-read format which includes all essential lines. Artist Transcriptions can be used to perform, sequence or for reference.

CLARINET

00672423	Buddy De Franco Collection	$19.95

FLUTE

00672379	Eric Dolphy Collection	$19.95
00672372	James Moody Collection – Sax and Flute	$19.95
00660108	James Newton – Improvising Flute	$14.95
00672455	Lew Tabackin Collection	$19.95

GUITAR & BASS

00660113	The Guitar Style of George Benson	$14.95
00672331	Ron Carter – Acoustic Bass	$16.95
00660115	Al Di Meola – Friday Night in San Francisco	$14.95
00604043	Al Di Meola – Music, Words, Pictures	$14.95
00673245	Jazz Style of Tal Farlow	$19.95
00672359	Bela Fleck and the Flecktones	$18.95
00699389	Jim Hall – Jazz Guitar Environments	$19.95
00699306	Jim Hall – Exploring Jazz Guitar	$19.95
00672335	Best of Scott Henderson	$24.95
00672356	Jazz Guitar Standards	$19.95
00675536	Wes Montgomery – Guitar Transcriptions	$17.95
00672353	Joe Pass Collection	$18.95
00673216	John Patitucci	$16.95
00672374	Johnny Smith Guitar Solos	$16.95
00672320	Mark Whitfield	$19.95
00672337	Gary Willis Collection	$19.95

PIANO & KEYBOARD

00672338	Monty Alexander Collection	$19.95
00672487	Monty Alexander Plays Standards	$19.95
00672318	Kenny Barron Collection	$22.95
00672520	Count Basie Collection	$19.95
00672364	Warren Bernhardt Collection	$19.95
00672439	Cyrus Chestnut Collection	$19.95
00673242	Billy Childs Collection	$19.95
00672300	Chick Corea – Paint the World	$12.95
00672537	Bill Evans at Town Hall	$16.95
00672425	Bill Evans – Piano Interpretations	$19.95
00672365	Bill Evans – Piano Standards	$19.95
00672510	Bill Evans Trio – Vol. 1: 1959-1961	$24.95
00672511	Bill Evans Trio – Vol. 2: 1962-1965	$24.95
00672512	Bill Evans Trio – Vol. 3: 1968-1974	$24.95
00672513	Bill Evans Trio – Vol. 4: 1979-1980	$24.95
00672329	Benny Green Collection	$19.95
00672486	Vince Guaraldi Collection	$19.95
00672419	Herbie Hancock Collection	$19.95
00672446	Gene Harris Collection	$19.95
00672438	Hampton Hawes	$19.95
00672322	Ahmad Jamal Collection	$22.95
00672476	Brad Mehldau Collection	$19.95

00672390	Thelonious Monk Plays Jazz Standards – Volume 1	$19.95
00672391	Thelonious Monk Plays Jazz Standards – Volume 2	$19.95
00672433	Jelly Roll Morton – The Piano Rolls	$12.95
00672542	Oscar Peterson – Jazz Piano Solos	$14.95
00672544	Oscar Peterson – Originals	$9.95
00672532	Oscar Peterson – Plays Broadway	$19.95
00672531	Oscar Peterson – Plays Duke Ellington	$19.95
00672533	Oscar Peterson – Trios	$24.95
00672543	Oscar Peterson Trio – Canadiana Suite	$7.95
00672534	Very Best of Oscar Peterson	$22.95
00672371	Bud Powell Classics	$19.95
00672376	Bud Powell Collection	$19.95
00672437	André Previn Collection	$19.95
00672507	Gonzalo Rubalcaba Collection	$19.95
00672303	Horace Silver Collection	$19.95
00672316	Art Tatum Collection	$22.95
00672355	Art Tatum Solo Book	$19.95
00672357	Billy Taylor Collection	$24.95
00673215	McCoy Tyner	$16.95
00672321	Cedar Walton Collection	$19.95
00672519	Kenny Werner Collection	$19.95
00672434	Teddy Wilson Collection	$19.95

SAXOPHONE

00673244	Julian "Cannonball" Adderley Collection	$19.95
00673237	Michael Brecker	$19.95
00672429	Michael Brecker Collection	$19.95
00672351	Brecker Brothers... And All Their Jazz	$19.95
00672447	Best of the Brecker Brothers	$19.95
00672315	Benny Carter Plays Standards	$22.95
00672314	Benny Carter Collection	$22.95
00672394	James Carter Collection	$19.95
00672349	John Coltrane Plays Giant Steps	$19.95
00672529	John Coltrane – Giant Steps	$14.95
00672494	John Coltrane – A Love Supreme	$14.95
00672493	John Coltrane Plays "Coltrane Changes"	$19.95
00672453	John Coltrane Plays Standards	$19.95
00673233	John Coltrane Solos	$22.95
00672328	Paul Desmond Collection	$19.95
00672454	Paul Desmond – Standard Time	$19.95
00672379	Eric Dolphy Collection	$19.95
00672530	Kenny Garrett Collection	$19.95
00699375	Stan Getz	$18.95
00672377	Stan Getz – Bossa Novas	$19.95
00672375	Stan Getz – Standards	$17.95
00673254	Great Tenor Sax Solos	$18.95
00672523	Coleman Hawkins Collection	$19.95
00673252	Joe Henderson – Selections from "Lush Life" & "So Near So Far"	$19.95
00672330	Best of Joe Henderson	$22.95

00673239	Best of Kenny G	$19.95
00673229	Kenny G – Breathless	$19.95
00672462	Kenny G – Classics in the Key of G	$19.95
00672485	Kenny G – Faith: A Holiday Album	$14.95
00672373	Kenny G – The Moment	$19.95
00672516	Kenny G – Paradise	$14.95
00672326	Joe Lovano Collection	$19.95
00672498	Jackie McLean Collection	$19.95
00672372	James Moody Collection – Sax and Flute	$19.95
00672416	Frank Morgan Collection	$19.95
00672539	Gerry Mulligan Collection	$19.95
00672352	Charlie Parker Collection	$19.95
00672444	Sonny Rollins Collection	$19.95
00675000	David Sanborn Collection	$16.95
00672528	Bud Shank Collection	$19.95
00672491	New Best of Wayne Shorter	$19.95
00672455	Lew Tabackin Collection	$19.95
00672334	Stanley Turrentine Collection	$19.95
00672524	Lester Young Collection	$19.95

TROMBONE

00672332	J.J. Johnson Collection	$19.95
00672489	Steve Turré Collection	$19.95

TRUMPET

00672480	Louis Armstrong Collection	$14.95
00672481	Louis Armstrong Plays Standards	$14.95
00672435	Chet Baker Collection	$19.95
00673234	Randy Brecker	$17.95
00672351	Brecker Brothers... And All Their Jazz	$19.95
00672447	Best of the Brecker Brothers	$19.95
00672448	Miles Davis – Originals, Vol. 1	$19.95
00672451	Miles Davis – Originals, Vol. 2	$19.95
00672450	Miles Davis – Standards, Vol. 1	$19.95
00672449	Miles Davis – Standards, Vol. 2	$19.95
00672479	Dizzy Gillespie Collection	$19.95
00673214	Freddie Hubbard	$14.95
00672382	Tom Harrell – Jazz Trumpet	$19.95
00672363	Jazz Trumpet Solos	$9.95
00672506	Chuck Mangione Collection	$19.95
00672525	Arturo Sandoval – Trumpet Evolution	$19.95

Prices and availability subject to change without notice.

0606

PLAY MORE OF YOUR FAVORITE SONGS
WITH GREAT INSTRUMENTAL PLAY ALONG PACKS FROM HAL LEONARD

Ballads

Solo arrangements of 12 songs: Bridge Over Troubled Water • Bring Him Home • Candle in the Wind • Don't Cry for Me Argentina • I Don't Know How to Love Him • Imagine • Killing Me Softly with His Song • Nights in White Satin • Wonderful Tonight • more.

00841445	Flute	$10.95
00841446	Clarinet	$10.95
00841447	Alto Sax	$10.95
00841448	Tenor Sax	$10.95
00841449	Trumpet	$10.95
00841450	Trombone	$10.95
00841451	Violin	$10.95

Band Jam

12 band favorites complete with accompaniment CD, including: Born to Be Wild • Get Ready for This • I Got You (I Feel Good) • Rock & Roll – Part II (The Hey Song) • Twist and Shout • We Will Rock You • Wild Thing • Y.M.C.A • and more.

00841232	Flute	$10.95
00841233	Clarinet	$10.95
00841234	Alto Sax	$10.95
00841235	Trumpet	$10.95
00841236	Horn	$10.95
00841237	Trombone	$10.95
00841238	Violin	$10.95

Disney Movie Hits

Now solo instrumentalists can play along with a dozen favorite songs from Disney blockbusters, including: Beauty and the Beast • Circle of Life • Cruella De Vil • Go the Distance • God Help the Outcasts • Kiss the Girl • When She Loved Me • A Whole New World • and more.

00841420	Flute	$12.95
00841421	Clarinet	$12.95
00841422	Alto Sax	$12.95
00841423	Trumpet	$12.95
00841424	French Horn	$12.95
00841425	Trombone/Baritone	$12.95
00841686	Tenor Sax	$12.95
00841687	Oboe	$12.95
00841688	Mallet Percussion	$12.95
00841426	Violin	$12.95
00841427	Viola	$12.95
00841428	Cello	$12.95

Prices, contents, and availability subject to change without notice.
Disney characters and artwork © Disney Enterprises, Inc.

Disney Solos

An exciting collection of 12 solos with full-band accompaniment on CD. Songs include: Be Our Guest • Can You Feel the Love Tonight • Colors of the Wind • Reflection • Under the Sea • You've Got a Friend in Me • Zero to Hero • and more.

00841404	Flute	$12.95
00841405	Clarinet/Tenor Sax	$12.95
00841406	Alto Sax	$12.95
00841407	Horn	$12.95
00841408	Trombone	$12.95
00841409	Trumpet	$12.95
00841410	Violin	$12.95
00841411	Viola	$12.95
00841412	Cello	$12.95
00841506	Oboe	$12.95
00841553	Mallet Percussion	$12.95

Easy Disney Favorites

13 Disney favorites for solo instruments: Bibbidi-Bobbidi-Boo • It's a Small World • Let's Go Fly a Kite • Mickey Mouse March • A Spoonful of Sugar • Toyland March • Winnie the Pooh • The Work Song • Zip-A-Dee-Doo-Dah • and many more.

00841371	Flute	$12.95
00841477	Clarinet	$12.95
00841478	Alto Sax	$12.95
00841479	Trumpet	$12.95
00841480	Trombone	$12.95
00841372	Violin	$12.95
00841481	Viola	$12.95
00841482	Cello/Bass	$12.95

Favorite Movie Themes

13 themes, including: *An American Symphony* from *Mr. Holland's Opus* • Braveheart • Chariots of Fire • Forrest Gump – Main Title • Theme from *Jurassic Park* • Mission: Impossible Theme • and more.

00841166	Flute	$10.95
00841167	Clarinet	$10.95
00841168	Trumpet/Tenor Sax	$10.95
00841169	Alto Sax	$10.95
00841170	Trombone	$10.95
00841171	F Horn	$10.95
00841296	Violin	$10.95

Jazz & Blues

14 songs: Cry Me a River • Fever • Fly Me to the Moon • God Bless' the Child • Harlem Nocturne • Moonglow • A Night in Tunisia • One Note Samba • Satin Doll • Take the "A" Train • Yardbird Suite • and more.

00841438	Flute	$10.95
00841439	Clarinet	$10.95
00841440	Alto Sax	$10.95
00841441	Trumpet	$10.95
00841442	Tenor Sax	$10.95
00841443	Trombone	$10.95
00841444	Violin	$10.95

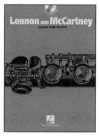

Lennon and McCartney Solos

11 favorites: All My Loving • Can't Buy Me Love • Eleanor Rigby • The Long and Winding Road • Ticket to Ride • Yesterday • and more.

00841542	Flute	$10.95
00841543	Clarinet	$10.95
00841544	Alto Sax	$10.95
00841545	Tenor Sax	$10.95
00841546	Trumpet	$10.95
00841547	Horn	$10.95
00841548	Trombone	$10.95
00841549	Violin	$10.95
00841625	Viola	$10.95
00841626	Cello	$10.95

Movie & TV Themes

12 favorite themes: A Whole New World • Where Everybody Knows Your Name • Moon River • Theme from Schindler's List • Theme from Star Trek® • You Must Love Me • and more.

00841452	Flute	$10.95
00841453	Clarinet	$10.95
00841454	Alto Sax	$10.95
00841455	Tenor Sax	$10.95
00841456	Trumpet	$10.95
00841457	Trombone	$10.95
00841458	Violin	$10.95

Sound of Music

9 songs: Climb Ev'ry Mountain • Do-Re-Mi • Edelweiss • The Lonely Goatherd • Maria • My Favorite Things • Sixteen Going on Seventeen • So Long, Farewell • The Sound of Music.

00841582	Flute	$10.95
00841583	Clarinet	$10.95
00841584	Alto Sax	$10.95
00841585	Tenor Sax	$10.95
00841586	Trumpet	$10.95
00841587	Horn	$10.95
00841588	Trombone	$10.95
00841589	Violin	$10.95
00841590	Viola	$10.95
00841591	Cello	$10.95

Worship Solos

11 top worship songs: Come, Now Is the Time to Worship • Draw Me Close • Firm Foundation • I Could Sing of Your Love Forever • Open the Eyes of My Heart • Shout to the North • and more.

00841836	Flute	$12.95
00841837	Oboe	$12.95
00841838	Clarinet	$12.95
00841839	Alto Sax	$12.95
00841840	Tenor Sax	$12.95
00841841	Trumpet	$12.95
00841842	Horn	$12.95
00841843	Trombone	$12.95
00841844	Violin	$12.95
00841845	Viola	$12.95
00841846	Cello	$12.95

0506